THE ELK POOL

DENNY MURAWSKA

outskirts
press

Outskirts Press, Inc.
http://www.outskirtspress.com

ISBN: 978-1-4787-7705-2

PRINTED IN THE UNITED STATES OF AMERICA

Acknowledgements

MANY THANKS TO my gifted family who helped with illustrations. That would include my sister and childhood fishing rival Kathy Potocki, son Tad Murawska, and first wife Karen Klinger. Gratitude goes out as well to Jennifer Langan, a fellow writer who did some typing and editing, and Zack Stanley for the haunting cover picture of a bobcat. Stop messing with those kitties Zack.

Table of Contents

Foreword

I KNOW DENNY began his life journey fascinated with nature. Even as a toddler, his folks nurtured his boundless curiosity, sparking an intense enthusiasm that drives him to this day. The family took English short-haired pointers they raised to field trials, where the thrill of chasing dogs on horses was a most anticipated event. Glorious weeks fishing in Minong, WI and went quail and pheasant hunting in the rolling cornfields of Morrison Illinois on the Schafer family farm, a stomping ground for four generations of Murawskas.

I met Denny when he was a freshman in college, and his thirst for the outdoors influenced me greatly. He taught me how to shoot a gun, showed me the best holes to fish, introduced me to protozoan life under the microscope, and allowed me to develop innumerable outdoor skills. I felt proud I knew how to fillet a fish, butcher a deer, chop wood, start a fire, and gather and identify wild mushrooms! I became a stronger and more well rounded woman honing these skills more often performed by men.

We developed a keen interest in Native American prose and poetry, and were awed by the vast knowledge of Native American traditions and struggles through Denny's graduate advisor, Dr. Bruce Von Zellen, a professor at Northern Illinois University. He introduced us to a Lakota Sioux medicine man named Selo Blackcrow who came to the college occasionally to talk about spirituality and native treaty rights. We internalized his influence, especially our views of nature, and let it inspire us throughout our lives.

Even as teens, both of us loved to write! Our mentor in high school was Dr. Rosemary Hayes, and we both became editors of our creative writing magazine. Den went on to be published in poetry magazines, outdoor periodicals, and ran a regular column in The Week out of Delavan Wisconsin for many years. These works often centered around his outdoor experiences. I went on to become a landscape watercolorist and gallery artist.

Denny often spoke about a transcendent experience he had during a pause from riding his motorcycle down the sand roads of Minong .In his late teens, alone in the deep woods, he felt a benevolent life force surrounding him. As they say, a veil was lifted. This immersion impacted his world view and later endeavors. Add to this a UFO sighting in 1975, again on Little Sand Lake near Minong, Wisconsin. Six of us watched as the unbelievable unfolded. Not long afterwards, we laid out the experience in the office J. Allen Hynek. Twenty years later, his predecessor Dr. Rodiguer became involved in some regressive hypnosis sessions, and somehow, this all ended up on television. The event and its implications were indeed life altering for all involved.

Oh, we've done some crazy and risky things together in the outdoors, and lived to tell the tale! We caught a 32 pound Northern Pike in Canada that I had to sit on top of all the way back to our fishing camp. We put together our own karate tournament, and got stuck in a blizzard in the White River National Forest of Colorado. I was cooking at an elk hunting camp that was ten miles up the mountain on horseback with our five month old baby, Tad. Denny rode up the weekend after it snowed! We became stuck in the middle of a pitching lake in Minnesota during a raging thunderstorm which was terrifying. We sampled mushrooms off cattle dung just to see if they would work their "magic." In time, we identified at least twenty-five varieties of edible wild mushrooms, sampling them all. Denny got sick only once, and it was severe! One frigid morning it seemed justifiable to cross a stream when the air was a frigid twenty degrees just to take a shot at a deer on the other side, and dragged another way after dark that ran off when shot with an arrow. We ate bear meat, tried to cook a squirrel once, and even had a one tough wild turkey for Thanksgiving. Denny started taxidermy when he was a high school teacher in Colorado, and his students would bring him animals to work on. I opened the freezer many a time to see frozen carcasses peering at me! I taught him how to initially paint fish, and we'd grind styrofoam in a blender to make forms that we mixed with plaster of Paris that became charged, and blew out of the blender and stuck to the ceiling like tiny white magnets.

What I'm trying to get across, is that this book is only a smattering of the many rich and flavorful moments experienced in Denny's life. I'm sure there will be more stories that will surface in the coming years, and he will be inspired by sharing this body of work with you. May you find it a joy to look at life through his eyes, and his heartfelt sentiments. It's been a family effort for some of it, and our son, his sister Kathy, and I contributed the illustrations. We hope you enjoy them as well.

May you revere nature, and spend as much time as you can in wild places. It's good for the soul.

Karen Klinger

Death is the only sleep
We truly awaken from.

Three Generations in the Wild

THE LONG, TAPERING tail feathers with their bold stripes stuck out from Dad's game vest like pliant swords. Both the cat and I watched with wide eyes as the gaudy, iridescent pheasants were plunked unceremoniously on the utility room floor.

I kneeled, inspecting each fowl closely. Several bobwhite quail were mixed in with the two cock pheasants. He had a good hunt.

Soon, the smell of steaming feathers would fill the house as each bird was meticulously plucked.

As the first of the lot was being dipped into the scalding water, I examined the remaining cock's scarlet eye patch. The eye was closed, but I had to pull down the lid to see its bright yellow stare once more.

After yanking out a few of the longest feathers for trophies, I placed them in a spot reserved for such treasures.

As I crawled into bed, I dreamed of the day when I would be able to tag along on the hunt.

Even before I could walk very far, I remember trips into the field to train our two English pointers. Our home was surrounded by undeveloped fields, and the dogs would always find and point a few pheasants. When I could no longer keep up, I rode on my father's shoulders, not wanting to miss any of the excitement.

As one dog would lock onto a scent trail, I could see their arousal. Body language spoke loudly, and it soon became easy to tell when the dogs were "birdy."

Like a hunting hound, I believe some of us are born with an instinct to trail and pursue game. Others remain, like a dachshund or frumped-up poodle, unmotivated by the whole thing.

For the truly smitten, almost anything can be hunted. Is it any wonder than many hunters are also fishermen? As a boy, there was simply no end to what I felt needed hunting. Frogs, turtles, snakes…anything was worth collecting. They were all trophies, and our home became a veritable menagerie as my sister joined in my zoological pursuits.

Three of my friends had fiberglass bows, and as early as third grade, we went afield in search of rabbits, squirrels, or anything that seemed like a worthy quarry. Most often, these creatures were as safe from us as if they were on another planet, but even then, the thrill was in the hunt itself.

At some point in each young hunter's life, there comes a moment of pure rapture when they find a BB gun under the Christmas tree. Usually, there are stern warnings about how and when to use this first gun. More often than not, they will be ignored from time to time. As an adult, I look back in shame at the countless frogs, sparrows and gophers that met their fate from a well-placed BB. I would not condone such behavior in my own son, but I somehow managed to get away with far more than I should have.

Trouble happened when our neighbor bit into her canned peaches and cracked one of her teeth on a BB embedded in the fruit. The bright yellow ones had seemed like nice targets to a second grader. At any rate, my family did not get along well with these people, so I can't remember getting in much trouble for that feat of marksmanship.

Around age 10 or 11, I was given my first shotgun. It was a beautifully engraved Italian single shot 20-gauge. Now, I was ready to really hunt.

As my father trained our pointers in the field with hidden pigeons, I was sometimes allowed to kill one so the dogs could retrieve it.

The countless hours of aiming my BB gun made this new firearm seem like an extension of myself. Knowing I had only one shot, I would often take a bit longer to concentrate before pulling the trigger. Perhaps it wasn't concentration at all. I simply brought the gun up, and game birds fell in a cloud of feathers, time after time. At that tender age, I rarely missed, and was quick to shoot.

Often, when birds were tallied at the end of the day, I had taken more than my father and uncles. It was a source of great pride, and I wish I could still shoot as well as I did then.

Throughout my teen and college years, the traditions of the hunt continued. Quail were always the most sought after quarry. To pursue them involved getting up hours before daylight, and taking a three-hour drive to the hilly countryside in western Illinois, on a farm my family has hunted for four generations.

Each night, before the quest, I could hardly sleep. By four a.m. I was wide awake, ready to sleep with the dogs in the back of the truck. In town, we would stop at a little cafe, loading up on stacks of pancakes and sausage. From there, it was a short jaunt to the briar-covered hills and hedgerows that we hunted all day long. As a youngster, I was so exhausted by the end of the day I could barely walk.

Lunch was savored in the crisp November air sitting alongside my uncle Bill's truck. Sandwiches, apples, and hot tea never tasted so good.

As the sun set, we always stopped at a ramshackle cider press to stock up on their homemade specialty. If ever the essence of an apple was bottled, it was in that roadside stand.

A thin old man attached to a constantly smoldering pipe smiled knowingly as he handed us this ambrosia. If you sipped it slowly, drawing a bit of air through it like a fine wine, nothing was better.

No small part of this chapter of my life was the camaraderie. At various times, the hunt was shared with my grandfather, my father, uncles, cousins and soon-to-be wife.

Even after most of the quail were gone, and the hunting but a shadow of its former grandiosity, I walked those steep hills and gulleys with my son. There was not much left to instill in him the excitement I once felt.

The heydays of abundant wild birds were over.

We kept in contact with the farmer from year to year. There were pheasants to be had, and wild turkeys have moved in with a vengeance, but quail are few and far between.

We have not hunted there for many years, and now, only my father and I are still able to walk those arduous fields. The dogs are gone, as are many of our hunting partners. Along with the quail, they remain only in our memories.

After seven years of college in the cornfields of DeKalb, Ill., it was time to get adventurous. As a beginning teacher with a young wife, the U-Haul safari to Colorado was quite a change.

The western slope of the Rockies cradled a dot on the map known as Collbran. This was hunting country, as in big game hunting and its beauty and remoteness was awe-inspiring.

For the next seven years, I spent every possible spare moment hunting and fishing. We were poor, but reveled in the sights and experiences around us.

My students frequently took me to their "secret" spots, behind locked gates that saw few hunters. It was common to have deer, elk and wild turkey walk within yards. Blue grouse, ducks and chukar partridge were abundant.

It was in this hunter's paradise I first picked up a newfangled device known as a compound bow. While primitive compared to today's models, it nevertheless hurled arrows with surprising accuracy out to 50 yards. I practiced with it until the tips of my fingers were numb and my shoulders ached. Over the years, that practice paid off by providing meat for the table and a lifetime of peak experiences.

Setting the sight pin of the bow on a deer at 15 yards was so much different than using a gun. Only a hunter can understand the level of excitement stalking a quarry with archery gear generates. It is a heart-pounding, breath-holding, shaky feeling when a bull elk or massive muley buck approaches to within bow range. Try as you might to remain calm, it is pointless.

I had read somewhere not to look into their eyes, that they could sense this. The scientist in me said no. The hunter averted his eyes.

I cannot recount all the experiences I enjoyed in those shining mountains. It would take volumes, and I must save a few for later.

After a divorce and return to the Midwest to be with my son, I felt totally alienated from the world I was thrust back into. Thankfully, my good friends granted me the run of the ranch during summers. I would also return each fall, when the aspens seemed to be luminous with golden yellow light.

It was a comfort knowing my spiritual "home" was still there, and I could sit behind the sage near a creek by the abandoned orchard. Here, deer would come to feed on downed apples, and one could always count on getting a close shot.

Even today, it gives me great solace to know I can always return there, and the mountains will seem the same. Bear and mountain lions still thread their way through the tangled creek bottom I once hunted and fished. Trout still rise to the hatch on Plateau Creek, and I survived the transition, remarried and prospered in spite of myself.

These days, I am fortunate to have access to several good deer stands. I am no longer poor, and can travel to exotic places to pursue my hunting and fishing. The rolling hills left behind by glaciers here in southern Wisconsin have their own special beauty. There were times when, living in the dry high desert, I had forgotten how green and full of life the land could be.

Wisconsin has been home for the past 17 years, and the small towns untouched by chain stores continue to hold a special place in my heart. The hunting and fishing is different here, but satisfying in its own way. My tree stands are nothing less than sacred spots to meditate in.

Picking my way through the woods at night or in pre-dawn darkness still gives that singular exhilaration. I imagine how a leopard feels as it heads out for the hunt. For in the end, those of us who hunt can rationalize what we do. We can show it is necessary to manage populations of animals.

In the long and short of it though, we hunt because we must. It is a passion, a drive, an instinct. For me, age has mellowed the urgency of filling a tag, bagging a limit, or holding out for a trophy. I have realized it is not necessary to spend every spare moment pursuing game.

I have discovered ways to enjoy the outdoors without hunting or fishing. Photography, riding my mountain bike and just hiking have become fulfilling. However, when opening day beckons, it is time to organize the tools of the hunt. Time to remember past outings and traditions. Time to remember the earlier inhabitants of the lands I hunt who left their stone axes, spear points and arrowheads underfoot. People whose spirits still roam these verdant landscapes.

My hunting buddies might refer to me as a "meat hunter." I have little interest in big racks or other such trophies. These days, I hunt less for meat than for memories of a perfect day. Whether or not I bag anything has become less and less relevant.

Perhaps what I hunt for is to, for a brief moment, experience the peak moments of the past, and knowing they have already been had. Catching my first wild trout on John Hill's ranch. Dropping that first game bird, a Hungarian partridge. Riding atop my father's shoulders, following the whir of a cock pheasant flushing underfoot and sailing into a place I can follow only in my heart.

Sermons in the Wild Places

THE OTHER DAY I read a saying on the website of a fellow fish taxidermist:

**"I'd rather be fishing and thinking about God
than sitting in church thinking about fishing."**

In my case, I suppose this would be true. While I fully support the values and spiritual messages conveyed in churches, they are not places where I feel closer to the Maker. Perhaps in the past, a congregation was a group of folks that knew each other on a first name basis and enjoyed giving praise through song and listening to scripture together. I honestly wish I were one of those who feel a spiritual "something" from this. The music and choirs can be moving. Sermons can be inspiring. Still, I have always ended up feeling awkward and self-conscious when in traditional church.

Apparently, congregations are reaching mammoth proportions. One that is featured on television fills a stadium with thousands of people.

These individuals appear so happy and moved by the sheer volume of like-minded fellow worshippers. I bet they represent all walks of life and races. It looks like a beautiful thing. It is just not for all of us.

I know there are others like me who turn to nature and silence for their spiritual communion. This is a matter of such importance to me, it can only be done alone. My pew may be an old stump, fallen log, or canoe. The stained glass windows appear as sunlight through a kaleidoscope of leaves and the changing colors of clouds as the sun sinks in the sky. Flowers call out to pollinators with their showy colors and heady fragrances. Something in them attracts us as well.

It is in such natural places one can experience "sermons" that are as varied as any in church. The cycles of birth, death, struggle, and prosperity are there around you, disclosing themselves in so many ways. Whatever the lesson, there is a common thread. It is a feeling of being surrounded by a great love that is revealed in the smallest, most trivial things. I cannot say how many hours I have spent since childhood walking beaches, deserts, and mountainsides searching for colored pieces of agate, carnelian, and crystals. Bags of fossils remind me always of the eternal yet changing nature of life.

A bug that was trapped in a piece of amber stares back at me from millions of years ago. The tooth of a fearsome reptile is a token of the eternal, creative force that God has endowed all life to inherit. Pottery shards and stone tools evoke imaginings of other ways humans have existed. How did the makers of these implements view their world and its creation?

It seems to me society views aloneness as a bad thing. We are encouraged to be gregarious creatures rather than loners. Yet, as I look at the lives of great spiritual leaders, it seems they knew when it was time to be alone. From Jesus to Thoreau, it was off to wild places to strengthen their spirits and clarify their thoughts.

THE ELK POOL

It hurts to be lonely, but not to simply be alone. I cannot be surrounded by the wind, trees, and babbling brooks and feel alone. The older I get, the less comfortable I am around throngs of people. It seems increasingly difficult to find opportunities to leave behind the noise and manic activity of society and find oneself in the company of birds and minnows. Alone in the company of unblemished creation, I can pray, sing, cry, or simply reflect and not feel silly or self-conscious. That is where church will always be for me.

Waxwing

LET ME SET the scene. A busy road coming out of a mall at the end of the work day. Cars whiz by. Suddenly, there is a bird in the road. A songbird. It was obviously struggling, and was soon to become a pancake. Drivers passed by without a second thought. One turned around and stopped in front of the unfortunate bird. Traffic had to stop as the bird was picked up and taken into her vehicle for examination. It was clearly stunned, but not bleeding or otherwise injured. It was a beautiful cedar waxwing. If you have seen one, you know. As the story goes, it was coddled and shaded on that hot morning. After awhile, it regained its sensibilities and proved it was able to fly. What a moment!

What is not mentioned here is that a "law" was broken. It is illegal to pick up or even touch songbirds and migratory birds. In some cases, it is a Federal offense. Fines for intentional violations can run from

$2000 to $5000 with perhaps nine months in the slammer. I know this because I am a fish taxidermist and have to abide by the letter of the "law." So, let us just say I may not be relaying a personal experience, but that of a very close friend.

This same close friend has told me about countless songbirds that slam into windows of her home. Sadly, some simply die. However, many are just stunned and need a bit of time in the cool shade away from marauding cats and dogs.Seeing them fly away is a true joy to behold, as I am told. Worthy of at least a few tears.

Statute 29.604 is quite laborious to read. The list of threatened and endangered plants and animals is nothing one is going to memorize. Would you recognize a Pecatonica River Mayfly? How about a Slender Madtom fish? If you wish to have a turtle for a pet, make sure is not a Blanding's turtle. This law's intent is admirable, but as with any law, its enforcement is open to the discretion of those who enforce it. If I am feeding birds in my yard, as many folks do, and a deer comes along to eat a few sunflower seeds, I could be in violation of game feeding and baiting rules.

As for me, if a bird hits my window, I will take care of it. If I see any creature in need of help, I will provide it. If I have to trespass to recover a wounded deer, that could well happen too. We can kill many species with impunity, but cannot touch others even when morality dictates it. We can feed some, but only those deemed worthy. Common sense and the heart must rule at times.

Saboteurs and Spoilers

LIKE MANY OTHER mammals, man can be a very territorial beast. We divide the world with lines signifying borders. The hunting woods are no different. You may think you have things all to your group, since you have a lease that was paid for, or just plain permission to hunt a zone that is clearly marked and posted. Sooner or later, you will run into a spoiler. Things can get heated when one party challenges the other's right to hunt "their" stand or woodlot.

My first experience with this was in the far southern part of the state many years ago. A prominent local family had always hunted a particular patch of woods surrounded by beans and corn. At one point, the aging farmer decided to lease to just a few men he knew and trusted.One of those was me. The patriarch of the pompous family ignored all trespass laws, and brazenly went in to hunt when he felt like it. Even after the local police were summoned, he continued to ignore the rule of law. One day on my stand, I got wind of a smell that was out of place. Mothballs! Someone during the night had snuck in and laced a few of our stands with mothballs in hopes we would be left with a spot that no deer would approach. At that point, I started looking for greener pastures, and found one!

A family whose kids were in my science class offered their family farm, smack dab in the middle of the suburbs for me to hunt. I was skeptical of the location, but it harbored many, many deer. One day after I had just settled into my tree perch, and I heard someone cuss. Then it came again. I homed in on a nearby tree, and there was another hunter not twenty yards away. He warned me to get out. Words and slurs went back and forth until we both came down to the ground, red-faced and confrontational. The claim was he and his friend had leased the farm for five thousand dollars. He seemed even more angry when I showed him a signed permission slip and indicated my lease was free. I insisted to settle this that we go the my friend's home and let him explain that his business partner had no right to lease out his family property. He read the interloper the riot act. It was tense, but they cleared out.

More recently, I got to my stand to find a truck parked right where I normally did. There was some old blood on the outside of the bed, and a fortune in beer cans being toted in the back.Judging by the brand, high rollers for sure. I wanted to surge into the woods myself, but decided to get the license number and call the county sheriff's police. Two officers arrived and told me it would be best to go wait some distance away. Each had an AR-15 and looked very serious. After a long wait, I discovered they were convicted felons and not supposed to have firearms. They were taken to jail. When asked if I wished to press charges, I declined.

You never know who you might meet in the woods. If they come at you and fire up a chain saw to claim "their" stand.......better have a quick way to avoid a bad fall! It has happened.

Pat and Zack

IT HAS BEEN roughly 41 years since I shared my classroom with two skinny, scraggly-haired boys who are now, of course, men. In the remote mountain town of Collbran Colorado, I had them as a captive audience for five years, learning the finer points of biology, chemistry, physics, and other courses I often invented. That is how things were back then. Our rustic little school still housed kids from kindergarten through their senior year. Back then, guns at school were not an issue. Walking down Main street with a holstered pistol never drew a second glance. They rested in the back windows of many pickups in the parking lot. Opening day of hunting season was an official school holiday, as it would have been pointless to teach when a large percentage of students were gone anyways. Tommy Lyons once set down his lunch sandwich long enough to bag a nice deer, in the middle of the football field. Being late for school was excusable if you were stuck behind a cattle drive. Primary school kids chewing Copenhagen tobacco, well now, that was a problem.

Pat and Zack were very bright students, and the three of us shared our passion for the outdoors. As was the local custom, we excelled in the art of trash talking each other about our hunting and fishing exploits. Mountain creeks that ran nearby seethed with feisty trout, and of course mine were always puny compared to what they caught. So I was told. Their bucks and elk made mine look like sheep. Yes, it was hard to be an easterner trying to man up to a western environment. I did all I could to impress upon them my worthiness as a savvy outdoorsman, but they always trumped me with something. All my students were aware I also taught karate at a nearby government facility. It was generally rumored I was pretty fast. One day, a challenge was issued. If I thought I was so fast, perhaps I could set off a muskrat trap before it caught me hand. Of course, I replied to the affirmative. The next day, they jangled into class with an ominous looking device. There was no way to back out and save face. The trap was set and I did my darnedest to snap my hand in and out before it bit me. Well, it nabbed me and it hurt like hell. I bit my lip and went at it a second time. Bingo! I did it! My self-esteem meter rose rapidly. Ha, if only they could see what I could do with my pistol.

One opening day of elk archery season, I invited Zack to join me on a trip up around Baxter Creek. I had a secret plan. He would "bird dog" and area where I had previously seen elk, and maybe flush a few in my direction. It worked like a charm! Young Zack seemed dumbfounded to see a "flatlander" sitting on a downed elk a few hours later. Of course, I explained it was due to my uncanny marksmanship and stalking skills. I reminded him of this frequently, and insisted he refer to me as "Opening Day Murawska." I even had a good chuckle the night they graduated from high school. During an awards ceremony, I presented each with a plaque commemorating their angling skills.I glued some dried sucker minnows on a couple of wood slabs, and cited to the audience their laudable achievements in the realm of "trash fishing."

We have kept in touch over the years, mostly e-mail. It was almost 22 years before we were to meet again on our home turf. Both were now successful government engineers, using their backgrounds to regulate precious water resources in a land that can be harsh and very dry. The wily desert rats are still at it. When this old teacher arrived in northern Arizona, it was time for a tour lead by mountain man Zack. We headed out across the desert hauling a seventeen foot boat across the desolate, but awe-inspiring arroyos and sculpted sandstone. After a two hour drive averaging about six miles per hour, we came upon a remote access point to Lake Powell. We basked in the 105 degree heat while almost filling the boat with striped bass and an occasional smallmouth. Surrounded by towering red sandstone walls, we savored the moment, and the unearthly silence that was not once interrupted by another human. Few would be crazy enough to haul a boat into this spot, even if they knew the place existed.

The next day, it was off on another desert road trip to a place where fossil shark teeth, Anasazi ruins, petroglyphs, and all sorts of good-ies beckoned. Sure enough, we had not stepped more than a few feet from the truck when fossil teeth began showing up. Here, on top of a mesa not far from the fabled ruins of Mesa Verde, we had a very real chance of stumbling onto sites of archeological interest that were still undiscovered.Shards of pottery with black and white designs gleamed all around. Flint chips showed where the ancient ones had worked their stone tools. In some canyons, we saw almost inaccessible dwellings perched on sheer cliff walls. Whether or not they had ever been excavated or even seen by the modern world was unknown to us. Carvings on rock walls showed desert rams, deer, bear tracks, and mysterious figures whose meanings remain indecipherable. I knew much of what we saw may not have been seen by another human for almost one thousand years, perhaps more. I will say we touched them, sat in the same spots, and gath-ered in the roots of humanity.

More recently, Zack and I took off again......not only to ancient ruins, but on an ATV adventure in the nearby San Juan mountains. We found many delicious mushrooms. On up over 12.000 feet, old uncle Denny was sucking for wind, but it was just a perfect day. Back down on the reservation, one of my favorite treats, mutton tacos. Lord if I could get these in Wisconsin! Oh to be back in my old stomping grounds, with my best friend. What a restorative experience!

I have lived. That is enough. To have times that bind me with my best friends, my past, the roots of human civilization, the dust of the ages........it is more than enough.

Mysteries of the Outdoors

MANY SCHOOLS OFFER programs in outdoor education. During these sojourns into nature, kids are instructed in orienteering, tree identification, forest resources and countless other activities that are meaningful and often fun. Having been involved in such trips for many years was a rewarding experience.

While it is true that teachers can convey a deeper appreciation of nature in their students through such expeditions, it is much more difficult to attempt this with a spouse.

On a recent trip up north to the Eagle River area, I decided to allow my dearly beloved Susan several opportunities to acquire a deeper rapport with some of the outdoor activities I am passionate about. Hunting with a bow, gun, and scrounging for wild mushrooms were on the curriculum.

The mushroom hunting was fantastic. On our first walk through the woods, I discovered a prize known as a "bear's tooth." This odd-looking mushroom is one of the most delicious of all edible fungi.

In a short time, Susan found an even larger one. Once she tasted the delicacy sautéed in butter, she agreed with all the authors of mushroom identification books that this was truly one of the best of the best. The wet and warm weather in the northern part of our state had left the woods full of goodies such as this waiting to be discovered. One morning, as if by magic, an entire flush of Boletus edulis popped up right in the back yard of her family cottage. It was as if some fairies had conjured them up just for us by magic. This prince of fungi is known as the King Bolete. It has almost as many names as there are European countries whose inhabitants relish it with a religious fervor. In all our miles of wandering, we never came upon another.

We collected enough to bring some back with us, to mix with wild rice for a gourmet treat beyond words. So far, so good!

I could feel the bonds between us growing stronger. Now came the real tests. Would Sue be willing to sit in a blind on an archery hunt far into the woods? How could she understand my fervor for this type of experience without actually being there?

I explained that it would involve two hours of silent sitting, waiting on a trail frequented by deer because of the abundance of acorns. Walking about the forest in pitch blackness is part of the thrill.

As luck would have it, as the sun sunk below the horizon, a doe poked her head up from a trail leading directly to our blind. At 20 yards, she was wary. Susan remained motionless in her camo headgear that made her look more like a terrorist than she knew. The doe stared directly at the blind, which she knew did not belong there, and was something new in her domain. As alarmed whitetails are prone to do, she stomped her foot, showing her alarm and alerting other deer in the area that something seemed wrong. There was a 10 minute staring match as she tried to figure out what this new addition to her forest was.

The doe cautiously circled downwind of us and started blowing as she caught our scent. This series of snorts is the final warning to every-thing in the woods that there was a problem here. It is also that last thing a deer hunter wants to hear. It is followed by the flash of an upraised white tail as the deer bounds off into the thicket.

Unless you are the adrenaline-pumped hunter, I am not certain squat-ting in a camo tent for hours is terribly exciting. Yet, once again, I felt Susan at least understood the patience and focus it takes to become obsessed with this type of hunting.

Finally, it was time to instruct my honey in the art of pistol shooting. As a boy, I had the good fortune to learn this difficult skill in a logical progression. It started with throwing clods of dirt in mock "wars" with armies composed of other kids in our neighborhood. From the start, I showed a knack for hurling projectiles and hitting targets. Yes, it was a dumb thing to do, but all the kids did it, so what was I to do? This quickly progressed to slingshots, BB guns, pea shooters and, finally, firearms.

Since Susan did not have a lifetime of these prerequisites, I decided it was time to jump in the pond and start from the top. My first concern was to provide hearing protection. Rather than waste an extravagant $2.39 on ear plugs, I brought along some toilet tissue. Heck, it had always worked for me. Perhaps it is why I often respond to questions by asking "what?" I could tell my would-be pistolero was ready when I noticed about five inches of white paper sticking out from the sides of her head like the half-cocked ears of a poodle.

I explained how to properly brace two hands on the grip of the gun and to take a wide stance. I did not tell her the pistol was loaded with

.357 magnum loads. This is not a beginner's round! Oh well, one has to start somewhere. The blast found my honey almost running away from this beast of a gun and shaking her hand up and down. While her hand position looked stable, I neglected to notice a finger just in front of the revolving chambers. You see, as one fires, a small amount of the blast is channeled out and onto anything in this area, resulting in a bruising powder burn. In addition, she complained of a terrible ringing in her head. Those magnum loads can be a bit much for a petite lady that is somewhat of a featherweight.

Well, I apologized profusely, and went through the old story about how one has to get back upon the horse and try, try again. It took plenty of coaxing, but I showed her how "expert" marksmen sight in their guns. You need a rest that gives a bit, like a sandbag. Since we had none, I improvised by wadding up her new parka on top of a Coleman cooler. Now she had a nice, stable rest.

Kaboom! Kaboom! Two shots rang out, both missing the paper plate target at 10 yards. At this point, Susan mentioned in a trembling voice that she might be more inclined to enjoy this endeavor a bit more with a much smaller gun.

It was at that point we noticed that her off-white parka now had several powder burns of its own. Oops! That was a $20 mistake on the part of her "mentor." He almost instantly agreed to replace the gun rest with one of equal value, or face some long moments alone in the forest for the next week.

These misadventures all ended on a happy note. By the end of the week, my able student was riddling her target with .38 special rounds. I noticed she had picked up a wing feather of a wild turkey found on one of our many walks, and held onto it like a prized ornament. She marveled at the colors of the trees, now at their peak of splendor. In the somber peace of the deep woods, we both soaked in the cathedral-like world enveloping us. What I had experienced so many times, she was now seeing with the eyes and heart of a child for the first time. In spite of her teacher's well-intentioned blunders, we had grown just a bit closer.

We are all sentenced to death
The price of life

The Floppy Doe

IT HAS BEEN many years since we stayed in our cabin on Duck Lake in Eagle River. The winding road along the chain of lakes has always been dotted with cabins. People being what they are enjoy the many deer in this relatively protected haven. Of course, many of these deer are fed. Some are so tame they will come and eat right out of a bucket. Having habituated themselves to humans, they wander the area at all times of day, and seem relatively unconcerned about being hunted or harassed in any way. The biggest danger to these creatures is traffic.

I first spotted one of these casualties one day while taking a walk foraging for mushrooms. A rather large doe appeared, and I could see one of its front legs just dangling uselessly and flopping around as she walked. I was immediately sorrowful for the animal, and wondered what mishap would have led to what appeared to be a horrible condition. I could only imagine the pain and suffering it must have been in. One thought was to report the poor thing to the DNR and have them put it out of its misery. It was a real heartbreaker. I then pondered taking control of the situation with my archery equipment at hand and the season open. However, I was certain it would horrify many of the numerous cabin dwellers. Heck, it could have ended up on somebody's front lawn.

Over the course of a few days, I saw the "floppy doe" a number of times, each one a gut-wrenching experience of wondering how much pain an animal can tolerate and still somehow carry on. One morning I encountered the neighbor next door and began relating the sad story of the afflicted doe. He immediately affirmed that he was familiar with this particular animal. What he related to me came as quite a shock. Evidently, this deer had been limping around the area for quite some time. In fact, it produced a fawn in the spring and raised it just as any fit mother would. I was dumbfounded! All my initial visions of a life of agonizing pain and misery inflicted on this unlucky creature were blown away like smoke from a campfire.

Thicket

Like a deer, shot through the vitals
I run on
Stumbling, bleeding
With no idea where to go

Except down well-worn paths
I have known forever
Diverging at the last moment
To a thicket vaguely remembered
There in the shadows
Kicking my last
Eyes wide.

Cane Pole

THERE ONCE WAS a time when simple tools and materials dominated our world.Long before the days of high modulus graphite, titanium, and even fiberglass, man fished with materials from the natural world. Bamboo rods, silken lines, hooks of bone....these things all go way back. I know because I go way back. Think Paleolithic. As I have inherited boxes of black and white photos from my youth, I remember well the small boy in the pictures. Shielded from the withering sun in my giant straw sombrero, I recall fondly the days of fishing with a cane pole.

While some may scoff at these whip bamboo rods as being kid's stuff, the truth is far more complicated than a skinny rod used to jerk panfish from their tangled lairs. Properly set up, cane poles can be used in placed and under situations that will make fly anglers and spinning rod snaggers cry in frustration.

The beauty of pole fishing is its simplicity. Any kid can do it with almost zero frustration. Yank 'em out of the pond, re-bait, repeat. At some point, young anglers may graduate to spinning gear or even fly fishing. It then seems reverting to a cane pole would be a childish thing to do. How wrong that is! Casting into shore from a boat most often leads to snags on vegetation right next to shore where linkers often lie under the slop.

Another way of stalking wary fish is to wade or use a float boat to get right up to the tight, weedy spot or brush pile and drop your bait straight down into a honey hole. This works fine for fishing shallow areas too thick with algae to drag a lure through. Crawling on your belly up the bank of a clear trout stream has all the drama of of stalking a big buck.

Here in the Driftless area of Wisconsin, we have some great trout streams, but many are a nightmarish jungle to cast into.A technique known as "dapping" involves taking a fly and making it dance over a productive pool, only now and then touching the water with it. Works with a cane pole as well. Ideally, you present your offering in a spot impossible to cast into, and are rewarded when a fish explodes to inhale your fly.

Bass anglers often use a sweeping technique to grab the attention of a big bruiser. Using just a few feet of line on the end of a pole, a noisy, gaudy lure can be swept right up along a bank or shallow weed edge. Crappie enthusiasts know the value of dabbling a live minnow or jig into a woody brush pile that is probably decorated with scores of hooks, bobbers, and crank baits. Sometimes, there is no more effective way of extracting panfish from their lairs.

Adults take this whole pole fishing thing much more seriously. In Europe, where carp fishing has been venerated as an art, high tech carbon poles that can reach over 42 feet in length are employed against wary species. It is catching on in the United States as well. If you think this is kid's stuff, check out the pricing on some of these monster poles like Daiwa's Yank 'N' Bank Pro model.Even large saltwater quarry like grouper can be caught on simple poles.

For me, I will stick with real cane on small ponds and streams just as I did as a youngster.It is the kind of fun that still brings out the child in me.

Turnip
Humble of the earth
Tasting of it
With butter, herbs, and cream
So far above it all.

The Head

On those days
When I could still hear the voices of trout
Discussions at a meeting place of birds
I often stared at the Viking head in the stream

A green-haired stoic
Jutting his whiskered jaw into the current
Mouth slightly ajar
Lying in motionless stealth
Waiting for a potato of a rock to crunch

For some reason
The lonesome head seemed stuck there
Lacking much of a body
Cracking logs and canoes against his brow
Grasping with swishing arms that fiercely foamed
Never smiling even to his companion
The rhinoceros
Whose horn poked up from the water
Just a bit downstream.

Caviar for the King

HAVE YOU EVER gutted a trout or perch bulging with eggs? Sure you have. They get discarded with the rest of the innards, right? Oh what a mistake! While the term caviar refers to a high brow version of sturgeon eggs produced in Russia, many varieties of fish eggs can be made into this gourmet treat. It could not be simpler, quicker, or more satisfying. As a fish taxidermist, I have often received fish flopping fresh from the ice shanty. While fresh fish is always best, once it is frozen before gutting, the fish eggs can turn into mush. So don't freeze it!

Fish egg sacs are covered in a membrane. Extracting them from the membrane is the only tricky part. Soak the mass of eggs in a brine solution. This can be 6 cups cold water to 1/3 cup of non-iodized salt. It penetrates quickly and makes membrane removal easier, and the eggs tougher. Surgically slice the membrane in a line down one side of the mass. The dull side of a knife can be used to scrape eggs off very carefully into another bowl of brine. Bits of membrane can them be removed by hand, and the eggs carefully strained. Another method is to lay the sliced mass on a wire screen. Anything with as small as a quarter inch opening works. Run some cold water over this under a little pressure, and it helps the eggs come loose.

Let them rest refrigerated in the brine around an hour in the fridge. Drain and rinse. Some folks add a bit of olive oil at this point, but is is not necessary.

Take a small taste. If too salty, distilled water can be used to draw some of the salt out just by rinsing through a strainer a few times. Really good caviar is not overly salty as is commonly believed. An example of this would be "lumpfish" caviar sold in most stores. It is from paddlefish and looks black. Not my favorite. If you love sushi and sashimi, you may have had salmon eggs or "ikura" which are my favorite. The large, orange, eggs can be popped one at a time into your mouth to savor heaven, or by the spoonful. If there was one food I could live on forever, this would be it. Supposedly a healthy baby food as well. We've all heard the benefits of fish oil touted. Well, these little baubles are full of it. Whether served on a bit of bread, a bagel, or straight up, they are irresistible. My favorite presentation is on a small square of seaweed wrap, or nori which is readily available in larger grocery stores. I have used eggs from pike, perch, trout, and salmon. Plenty of room to experiment here. In my German family, each New Year's Eve we made pickled herring, and cured the tiny sacs whole along with the fish. The mythology behind this was, the more eggs you eat, the more money you make in the New Year. Yeah, livin' the dream!

Bon Apetit!

My Mom

MY LIFE OF outdoor adventures could not have been possible without the examples my folks set. While most of the hunting trips were with Dad, Mom was always there for the fishing, and encouraging me from the onset to investigate the natural world.

Many of my earliest memories involve being close to Mom. At times, she was planting flower bulbs. Money was tight, and the bulbs were dug and saved for planting in the spring. Our backyard was large one. There was always a garden where I was shown how to dig rows along a string for planting. On shopping trips, Mom always returned with a new book, often a nature series. I digested each one with gusto. I remember how Mom made reading exciting. A book called "Color Kittens" stands out. She would read a page, then dramatically change the intonation of her voice as she quickly flipped the pages to colorful new visions. Often, I laid on the hardwood floor of my folks bedroom as Mom ironed. I would sit and draw, or read right under the ironing board. The room was made of knotty pine, and each pattern of knots in the wood had me imagining ghoulish faces were watching me. It was okay. Mom was there.

THE ELK POOL

Bass fishing on a private lake near Minong Wisconsin was always a thrill. My Dad got a week off each year from bricklaying, and we all anticipated our time in the north woods. Mom loved to fish, and was good at it. We hauled heavy stringers from the clear, spring-fed water, as well as from nearby Little Sand lake, which was only steps from our private paradise. The fresh fish were prepared right after my Dad cleaned them, and were relished by all. To this day, Mom does not understand catch and release. Just a waste of time as she sees it.

Mom's are known to be nurturing beings. Mine was exceptionally so. Both my sister and I had a penchant for housing animals of every description, both domestic and wild. I find it necessary to list just a few. First, the more conventional pets. Dogs, cats, birds, turtles, and goldfish. Next we have horned lizards, baby alligators, boa constrictors, garter snakes, guinea pigs, hamsters, ferrets, quail, frogs, mice, and a rat. This zoological collection fed a lifelong passion for living things. I have been shown an essay I wrote in fifth grade that tells of an ambition to be a biologist. That passion has never wavered.

Mom kept an extensive photo collection of our youth and travels. My folks took us to Coal City Illinois at a time when it was easy to find bags full of fossil ferns. It was such a thrill to tap the edges of hotdog-shaped rocks until they split cleanly to reveal treasures trapped inside. Museum trips to Chicago's Field Museum and Shedd Aquarium were frequent. There was so much to marvel at.In a recent discussion with my sister Kathy, it was brought up that my folks were kind of liberal with us. They allowed us to do things that we would certainly find borderline if we had to apply it to our own kids. We understand now that cell phones, GPS trackers, and smart phones are just new-fangled gadgets, that do not necessarily make the word a safer place. Long bike rides that lasted the day were mentioned, and hopefully, we came home fine. Handing a twelve year old a .22 rifle was probably a mistake, leading the mass extinction of gopher populations in the vicinity of our vacation cabins. Hopefully they made a comeback.

In college, I demanded a private room, and my folks popped for it. Mom made some lovely drapes and a matching bedspread for me, and of course I was the envy of the study floor. She was used to taking Simplicity patterns and making clothes for herself, so this was all second nature. Every nickel was saved. When money was tight, Mom went to work, mostly for my uncle who owned a print shop. There was never, ever any complaining that I remember. If I got in trouble at school, she was there to argue my case and always won. After an unexpected divorce, I had to return to Illinois from Colorado. The pain of this was excruciating. It was back to the flatlands to try to be a father to my young son. I was welcomed back to live in the house I spent most of my youth in. There, I was spoiled rotten as I had always been.

As an adult I can look back and see many of the things I took for granted were luxuries befitting a king. My laundry was always pressed, right down to my underwear which was folded neatly into the "tighty whitey" drawer. I never knew what a dirty house was. I know now. I enjoyed playing sick, and spent frequent days at home shooting my BB gun at plastic animals. When it was time to fill in my practice hours on the trumpet for my music teacher, she signed off for practices that never happened.

My mother never gave up on me. I still get frequent reminders on how I could dress up more, cut my long hair, and especially get rid of my beard. More good things would manifest themselves if I spent some time in church. While all of these things could happen, they probably won't. Especially the beard.

As I write this, Mom is ninety one years old. In just the last years, she has slowed down and settled into a small apartment with my Dad. Still, I remember a picture of my Mom with me as a very tiny boy. A former student of mine saw the picture in another article and said "Wow, your Mom was hot!" I guess it is fair to say that, yes, she was beautiful, and remains so.

Brushbuster

MANY WELL-MEANING SOULS have counseled me not to live in the past. I pretty much ignore most of what they say. The past defines who we are, where we have been, and how we came to live in the present. So it is with painted images. In my home, I have many original paintings from family members. Several of those closest to my heart were painted by my father. As a child, I remember a wooden box full of tubes of oil paints, linseed oil, and brushes. The smells I recall are as fresh as they were when I watched Dad sketching on a canvas, then applying the pigments that brought outdoor scenes to life. He was not a trained painter, yet his knowledge of flushing birds allowed him to portray moments in time that we shared. I tried to copy what he did. Mallard ducks were a favorite subject. I still have some drawings I made as a young child based on intently watching Dad sketch them out.

One painting stands out from the others, a flushing covey of quail. The scene is a reminder of many, many days of hunting the hilly bluffs near Morrison Illinois. These were days when quail were abundant, and our pointing dogs could locate four or five coveys each day. Those of us who lived those days cannot forget the heart-pounding excitement generated by the whirr of wingbeats rocketing out from dense brush. While I engage in many types of hunting and fishing, nothing comes close to the exuberant, startled, pure thrill of busting a covey.

Nowadays, the hedgerows of multiflora rose and briar filled valleys have been cleared out for the most part. The quail are not present in any great numbers. The farm we hunted for generations has been sold. My father is eighty-seven years old, and hobbled with knees that will not allow him to roam these hills anymore. He has already handed me his Browning shotgun that downed so many birds, knowing he cannot walk those hills and gullies anymore. He used to be the brush buster, burrowing through the gnarliest brambles with his leather-faced pants to kick out the stubborn single birds. He would root around places even our pointers would shy away from. I generally took the easier path, waiting for a shot opportunity after Dad did the dirty work.

No, I cannot live in "mindful" meditation locked into the present moment. More often than not, I gaze at old pictures and paintings of times gone by. I am not a Buddhist monk. I am a hunter. I enjoy shooting game, cooking it, and eating it. There is a spiritual aspect of taking this wildness into my own body. Some day, I can only hope my ashes will feed the plants in some special niche of this world where the birds and deer will infuse my molecules into their own, and some young hunter will experience the thrills of the hunt, and carry on traditions we hold so dear.

The Brushbuster
Portrait of Memories

The Brushbuster & Tad

Bobwhite Explosion Morrison, Illinois
- Painted by Dad

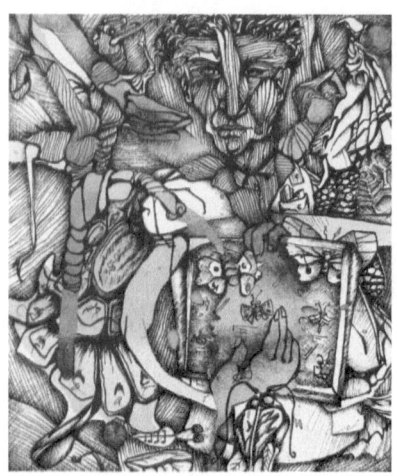

Top Ten Excuses for Mr. Warden

10. Of course I know the regular season is over, but the locals here told me we are now into the "farmer's season."

9. No, I am not hunting past legal hours. This is how coon hunting is done. (Grandpa actually used this one.)

8. You say hawk, I say buzzard.

7. Pretty sure market fishing is protected by a constitutional amendment.

6. Bait pile? No way! I decided to be proactive and plant next year's food plot now.

5. I made an honest mistake. Do you realize how much a horse resembles a cow elk through a night vision scope?

4. Look, I am not trying to be a smartass, but do you have some-thing against guys from Illinois hunting in Wisconsin? Flatlander is a demeaning term and most unprofessional. I will talk to you supervisor about profiling honest hunters.

3. If this is the United States, one license should cover the whole country.

2. So what if my blood alcohol is twice the legal limit. According to the rule book, party hunting is legal in this state. Like party?

And, the number one thing NOT to say to any warden......

1. I once aspired to be a warden, but my folks encouraged me to attend college. The mental discipline helped me to get through my "asshole" stage.

Pistol Packing

I BEGAN MY own brand of concealed carry in Illinois long before it had the blessing of lawmakers. Luckily, I am now a Wisconsin resident and do not live close to the border, as I used to. Funny how many governors of that fine state ended up behind bars, while denying citizens basic rights. Looks like some got their just desserts.

In my many years of being a concealed carry proponent, some of the most important lessons in the fine art of being a pistolero came not from any courses I took or "how to" books. They came from my years as a student of martial arts, and fifteen years as a black belt instructor in two very traditional Japanese styles of karate.

In karate, which has been described as a "tree of slow growth", students who want to learn everything at once and very quickly get bored and weeded out in no time. It is only those who persevere the endless, repetitious training which joins mind and body into a formidable weapon. In traditional styles, there is no mention of weapons training early on. Mental and bodily control are hallmarks of traditional styles, which is very different than the mixed martial arts hodgepodge of today. In fact, each session of Shotokan karate began with students kneeling and reciting "Dojo Kun" or basically, rules which govern the school and training.

1. Seek perfection of character.
2. Be faithful
3. Endeavor
4. Respect others
5. Refrain from violent behavior.

Not much is said here about kicking butt or other violence-laced verbiage. In time, you learn that your mind is the source of your defense, and by extension, your body. Weapons training begins only when a certain mastery of this precept is evident to a competent, caring instructor. Whether the weapon is a wooden staff, sword, nunchaku, or the body itself, all involves an extension of a will cultivated to react in a refine manner.

There have been a number of times in life where I would have had every legal right to unleash the full force of my training on a would-be attacker, and several times a gun would have been appropriate as well. Thankfully, my training allowed a cool head to prevail, and nobody was harmed.

I feel good about carrying a gun because I know it is an extension of my will. I do not hang out in places that brood trouble, and avoid the types of people who look for it when I can. The most important lesson anyone can and should have embedded in their mind when it comes to guns, is intent. Have you practiced over and over and over with that weapon until it feels like an extension of your own body? Can you draw it and manipulate it in total darkness? Are you as familiar with it as your own hand?

Long ago, I learned to manipulate weapons by handling them constantly. This is not idle play. It is necessary. I do the same with my guns. As with physical fighting, confrontations are not sought out. However, if and when the time comes to use a gun, do you have the intent necessary to do so? Brandishing a weapon in hopes of "scaring" an attacker is dangerous and foolish. Have you developed the mindset of knowing that, if the time comes, you can simply draw on training and experience to pull the gun to use it, without any flourish or fanfare? That is what it takes! In karate, I learned that if I got within arms length of an opponent, IF I initiated the first strike, I would most assuredly hit exactly what I wished to with devastating force. It is a matter of human reflexes and how fast one can react. One does not crouch into a Karate Kid crane stance and start flapping wings of death to scare a would-be attacker. Similarly, one does not brandish a weapon hoping to scare the bad guy. You train to act almost reflexively, and very deliberately, without hesitation if a self-defense situation emerges. As one instructor put it, " action almost precedes thought."

So, practice repetitiously. Know you will hit your mark within a certain range. Be able to manipulate this tool in your hand as an extension of your body and will. Know you have the attitude ingrained in you to use it if the need arises, and live with that confidence. Some of the most accomplished pistoleros in the Old West were not always the fastest. They were the most deliberate.

Butcherstrap

ONCE UPON A time in a young teacher's life, I used to carve up my own deer. There are those who are quite adept at this, and prefer to do it themselves. I was never one of those butchers. The deer was plopped onto the kitchen table with a tarp under it, then whacked and hacked. Cuts were not identified as chops or steaks. Just chunks and more chunks. I did not even have a grinder, so smaller bits were labelled "chili." As my wealth grew, I was able to take my venison to a locker plant and have it done properly. As I grew even older and more affluent, I began to wonder if maybe I was getting all my meat back. A few outfits were reputed to short shank a person, so to speak. Others had stellar reputations as to honesty.

Having fed on wild game most of my life, I still have a penchant for flavorful meat. Some might call it gamey. I call it tasty. At any rate, I now hunt the coulee regions around Taylor Wisconsin. Get into the back country far enough, and you run into many Amish homesteads. I put out the word that I was looking for mutton. Not lamb, but a mature, full-bodied sheep. I first tasted mutton on the Navaho reservation in New Mexico where I was visiting a former student and best friend. There was something about eating mutton tacos below the imposing red sandstone pinnacles that was sensual for me. As luck would have it, I purchased a very mature sheep and had an Amish fellow butcher it for me.

As I loaded the carcass into the bed of my truck, I could see the clean, superb job that was done on it. I was handed a plastic bag that I was told contained the heart, liver, and butcher strap. Now we have all heard of loin, tenderloin, backstrap, and other cuts of meat. Butcher strap? I was assured it was small, but the most succulent and prime piece of meat on the animal. So when I arrived at home, I opened the bag. There was the heart and liver alright, but nothing else. Nothing. Now we all know Amish folks are not capable of uttering a falsehood. I searched the floor of the truck, and any other place it might have fallen. It did not exist. I could not find any terms like butcher strap online. What had happened? I finally surmised I was the butt of an Amish joke. If you think of butcher's strap as in the possessive case, it was an honest way of saying he took it. A fairly common practice I am told. A gratuity if you will. I can only smile over this now. The butcher deserved his strap. I enjoyed slow cooked mutton shank for my birthday. Truly sublime.

Going Pink

FORGET FOR JUST a minute the presidential debates, global warming, and world terrorism. It appears Wisconsin is about to be the first state to legalize blaze pink camo. Can the end of civilization be far behind? In a tactical ploy to entice more women to put down the knitting needles and pick up a gun, some clever legislators figured blaze pink would be the ticket. You betcha! Of course, many women hunters are offended by this sexist conspiracy. Men, well, I am pretty sure are not buying into the concept. Imagine sauntering into deer camp with a pickup truck filled appropriately with Leinenkugel's beer wearing pink! While the beer will be appreciated, will old timers buy into the fact that you are also carrying a sequin embroidered duffel bag full of gear? Do you want to be the Liberace of Land O' Lakes? Imagine Burt Reynolds in the movie *Deliverance* sneaking up on those inbred rascals harassing his camping buddies. Would he wear pink? How about Doc Holliday at the OK Corral? (In truth, the sight might have caused the cantankerous Clantons to flee in fear.)

But wait! Is this just a bunch of liberals trying to even the playing field of gender issues? It appears that a clever professor from the University of Wisconsin has determined that, while blaze pink is equally as visible and safe as blaze orange, deer cannot see it as easily. Evidently, deer can see yellows quite well. Blaze orange is chock full of them. Blaze pink is not. Okay guys. Are you convinced now? Are you running for the hunting catalogs to stock up on pink accessories the moment you get done reading this? Better hit the craft store and spend the winter slack time embroidering hearts, butterflies, and rhinestones onto your new garb. You cannot accessorize too much. Pink guns are already the rage, but what about boots and gloves? Keep looking. Next season you need to be prepared.

Of course, you can "swing both ways" and attire yourself in a combination of blaze orange and blaze pink. While it may hint at a gender identity crisis, It will spare you a chunk of change. Your hunting buddies will be scratching their heads at this fashion faux pas. No matter what rationale you give for your idiosyncratic behavior, nobody is going to buy it. Pink camo is a gateway behavior that can lead to the demise of the deer camp. Imagine some dweeb in your camp sitting cross-legged with a wine glass full of pink Zinfandel, pinky finger appropriately extended. Yes, this will be the same fellow that flits around your cabin spritzing the air with breezy fresh aerosol following every belch and beer fart. After hours, he will sit around primping his nails with pink polish, and use a blush tone for face camouflage.

Is this the end of manly hunting as we know it? Will grunt calls of the future sound like Sarah Palin? Will deer decoys become alluring to bored hunters because of the long eyelashes and sexy turn of the head? I hope not. We stand at a crossroads. Will tradition prevail, or are we headed down the one-way road to an apocalypse?

Dawn

IN OUR WORLD of mandated work, sleep and wake cycles, there are far too few opportunities to soak in that special time of day known as dawn. On those days we have the luxury of not having to tramp off to a job, it is easy to simply roll over in bed and fall back to sleep, tired from another week of work. However, there is much to be missed by not rising early and greeting the first rays of sun.

First, there is a soul-stilling quietude. If you are near water, sliding a canoe into the mist hovering over tranquil waters gives a feeling of leaving the world behind. In this brief interlude between darkness and light, senses become magnified, and there is a feeling of a need to tread lightly and without noise.

Even the invisible makes its presence known. Spider webs gilded with dew sparkle in a thousand places. Shortly, they will sink back to invisibility. Fish that spend the heat of day skulking under cover are taking advantage of dawn, cruising shallows in search of prey.

Wildlife in general is easier to see during this calm. A stealthy approach may allow you a close look at a heron perched along some shoreline, statuesque and regal as it scans the glassy stillness for minnows. Deer use this time to feed and take a drink, so coming upon a doe with her fawn lagging behind is always a possibility. Animals every- where seem to be using this time to full advantage. They do not possess the luxury of using these hours for sleep. Chattering squirrels and chipmunks seem to chastise humans wandering through the early calm. They are going about their business, and would prefer to remain undisturbed.

Part of the hush during these peak moments comes from the fact that the air is still. Warming of the atmosphere to produce convection currents and a breeze has not yet begun, and so even the invisible cloak of gases surrounding one becomes more of a palpable entity.

However, all too soon, these same air molecules will begin to vibrate with sounds of automobiles, boats and ATVs, destroying the magic of day- break.

In a perfect world, I would reset my biological clock so as to be more in tune with the rhythms of life. Each dawn and sunset would be an event to behold and wonder at. I would get my chores done at some point, then nap like a cat whenever I felt the urge.

I guess this is why vacations can be so invigorating, and retirement so attractive. Most of our lives are spent living out of sync with what is natural. It has been calculated that Americans put in more hours of work than even peasants did in medieval times. A revered sage was once asked the secret of his wisdom. "I eat when I am hungry, and sleep when I am tired." Amen!

> First light
> Subtle, shadowless
> Not always a slab of bright orange
> A sigh.

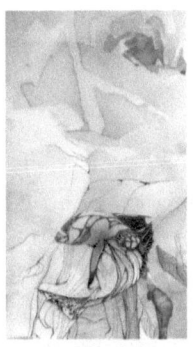

Sleeper

My eyes rose with the sun,
picking out soft whiteness
of her pouty-mouthed breathing
without a sound

Eyelids telling me no dreams
interrupted this rest
from thoughts that would soon come
pouncing catlike
to wild some part of her

Ideas flushing like game birds
carried her away

Soon forgotten
softness taking hold once more.

We live many lives
They happen all at once.

Anna

If you are among the lucky, at some point in your life, you meet a person who is a mirror of yourself. I am not talking about guys engaging in guy talk, bragging rights, or sports babble.

Parallels in the natural world

Looks and gender do not come into play. It is as if, from some parallel universe, this being appears in your life, and, bit by bit, you come to realize you share a scary number of traits, interests and instincts.

For me, this
person is Anna
Marie Fritz. We
both write for

Wishigan Outdoors, a magazine focused on hunting and fishing in northeastern Wisconsin. Our articles almost always run side-by-side. I could tell from reading her insights into nature that we think alike about many things. So, one day when she contacted me with a compliment on a piece in *Wishigan* magazine, I responded.

This lady has so many dimensions to her I don't know where to begin. As she puts it, she has an eye for "all things bright and beautiful." Mostly, these are snippets of the natural world that she preserves through her photographs, artwork and stories. I agree with her friends who describe her as a female counterpart of John Muir.

Like myself, Anna once did taxidermy for an avocation. She has worked as a journalist, painted signs, raised commercial poultry and entertained. I have a photo of a gig she had years ago where she shared the stage with Frank Sinatra.

Part of her life was spent "out West" toting a bright silver revolver and being quite a shot with it. A mountain ram she shot and mounted herself still glowers over her living room. We also share a hobby known as lapidary—the cutting and polishing of rocks to bring out their natural beauty. When she talks of her many hunting and fishing exploits, there is such an exuberance and passion in her tone. I get the feeling she has eaten just about every wild thing that swims, flies or crawls. Last deer season, she explained how she rendered the fat from a chunky doe to save for cooking doughnuts in. That is hardcore!

This summer, I got a chance to interview Anna while fishing up north. Immediately, I could see why she is known as the Lavender Lady. Rings, pendants, makeup—every adornment imaginable was some shade of purple. I was half expecting to see something like a reincarnation of Annie Oakley, but instead became acquainted with a very feminine woman. Her entire garden and fencing around it are shades of lavender as well, and her surreal photos of it turn up in her books.

These days, Anna has set down the guns, at least for a while, to write.

It is refreshing to be able to converse and share outdoor stories with somebody besides the boys. When Anna talks about the magic of watching small mouth bass rising for insects at her secret spot on a river, I understand. I know there are other women out there who share this passion for the woods and waters, but far too few.

One of my seventh grade students tells me of her keen anticipation for an upcoming hunt this year. She set a few of the boys straight about how to properly track a buck, and other rules of the hunt. I can only hope more young ladies will have such feelings nurtured by caring families, and share in the sublime pleasures of our natural world, far from the nearest shopping malls.

Tiptoe

On a hard night's sleeplessness
ever so lightly she came to me
bending to my ear
Not so much as the longed-for lover
she had been
but as a teasing friend

Wrapped tight to her, I could not remember
the words, or if there were any
Just the briefest touch of knowing where
I had been
who I was
and am

Unfolding youth
Layer upon layer

Ever young.

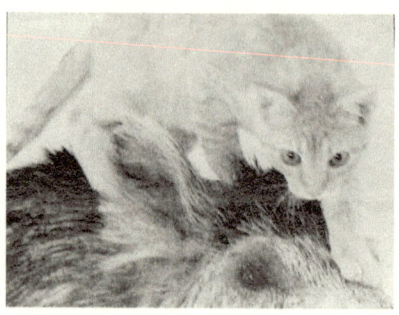

My Kitten the Panther

WHEN IT COMES to understanding why we hunt, cats can be art-ful teachers. They have no prescribed curriculum, state standards, or useless jumble of methodology to follow. Not surprisingly, they don't lecture very much. The eloquence of their body language is enough to remind us that hunting can indeed be an instinct.

We now live with a kitten separated at a tender age from her mother. She is a hunter by birthright. It is all fun and amusing to watch. This world of imagination reminds us as adults how we also went through this romping stage of life. Peek-a-boo, hide and seek, and a cornu-copia of other behaviors played out in our world were just plain fun.

Now, somewhere along the line, parents generally intervene to teach us refinements of how to play. Boys often are encouraged to partici-pate in behaviors different from those of girls. At least in my neigh-borhood, target-oriented play was tolerated, just as is the play of a feisty kitten. Most young males toyed with pea shooters, slingshots, primitive bows and eventually BB guns. We roamed the forests and fields, emulating our fathers on the hunt. We flailed our mostly use-less projectiles at whatever we decided was worthy game. This was all kitten play.

Somewhere between the days of shameless chucking of rocks at frogs, and taking my first deer with a bow, I became an adult. Questions arose within as to why I had such a passion for what some disdain as bloodsport.

We humans are a bit more complicated than kittens. Nature and nurture come into play. Fortunately, I am ultimately grateful that the instincts that still burn in me were nurtured. Too many children have had this "educated" out of them to the point where they really do not understand the source of our survival. While they cheerfully munch animals turned into patties and sausages, they understand little of the source. It remains as simple today as in prehistoric times. Life eats. Survival of the living depends on the hunting or gathering of life to be eaten.

As a teacher, I have often been shocked at how scant the knowledge of where our food comes from is understood by most children. Many have never experienced the joy of planting and harvesting food crops. Some do not know peas come from a pod. A kohlrabi is as foreign to them as a flying saucer. Wild berries and mushrooms are fearsome objects to be avoided at all costs.

And, when it comes to killing animals, well, it is just wrong, cruel and gross. Our meat and daily bread bear no resemblance to the sources they came from.

Eating a bag of fries is tasty, but not as inspiring as taking a pitchfork and digging a bucket of potatoes you grew yourself from a tiny "eye." The sublime flavor of a wild morel or tangy beefsteak mushroom foraged from the woods bears scant resemblance to the watery, lifeless slices floating in a jar to be flopped on a pizza.

As humankind shifted from a hunting and gathering form of life to a more predictable farming and herding of domestic creatures, the skills of the hunter were less and less needed for survival.

These skills, once deemed necessary, became "sport." It is a term I disfavor, as it is so much more complicated and visceral than some other things we call sport. Over the years, as I have mused just why I find so many reasons to hunt, fish and forage, I cannot downplay the role of instinct. How is it so many of our "sports" involve the lobbing of some projectile at some goal?

Whether it is a target, hoop, ball or hole in the ground, is it just chance we do these things for recreation? Was there not a time when the goal and targets were all living things we ate?

Now, as I grow nearer the age of 60 than 50, I have grown to understand my passions. They are reflected in the eyes and antics of our kitten. As she will someday settle down a bit and mature into a cat, so have I. The old instincts remain intact. I still peer into creeks, farm ponds and forest clearings, wondering what lies therein. It is still fun to toss fuzzy bugs from a fly line to see what might lurk below the water. Drawing an arrow across a bow while eye to eye with a deer still makes my heart beat like nothing else.

However, there is no more obsession to fill a tag or score a limit. The goal of my wanderings is more to experience nature than to fill a tag or score a limit.

Cold mornings feel just a bit colder. The work of tilling and weeding hurts my cranky joints. Still, there is the marvel of unexpected treats that reveal themselves in my meanderings. While I no longer have to hunt or forage or farm to survive. The freezer is filled with smoked hams, steaks, and sausages made from lean, healthy animals I have hunted.

As the air turns a bit cooler, other signs foretell the end of summer. Once again, vague stirrings within remind me the time of the hunt is nearing.

> I cannot love my neighbor as myself
> Since I have a cat I love much more.

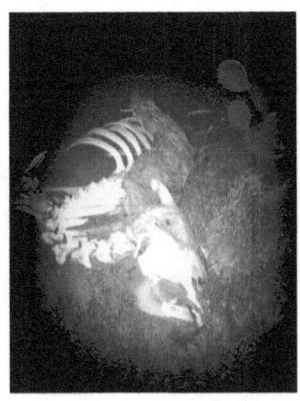

Leopard

My name is Leopard
the night is mine
I make no sound, no track, no sign
I am an essence
a dark spotted ghost
Night is my doorway
your village, my host

The scratch on the roof
Is it branch?
Is it breeze?
Or the ember-eyed shadow
come down from the trees.

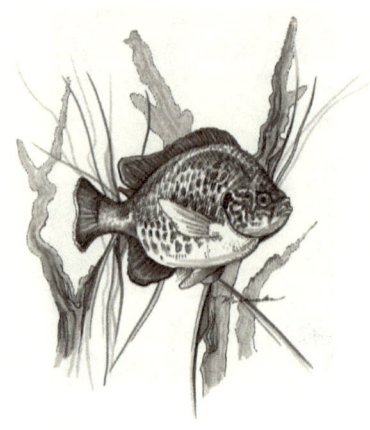

Songs to Hunt by

"HI HO, HI HO, a hunting we will go!"

For those of us who head into the woods and fields each fall to hunt, autumn is a special and sacred time, given to the wonder and ritual of deer camp. Seasons begin even before it feels like fall. The air is still warm, farm markets are full of the striking forms of pumpkins, gourds, displaying the fruits of the earth transformed from whispers of air, water, and sunlight into sustenance we rely on. There is no certain day when autumn begins. One morning, the soybeans seem to have been magically touched by gold. Sumacs begin to reflect crimsons not there the week before. Bracken ferns have browned, even while most trees retain their vibrant greens of summer. Something has changed, and one day, upon venturing out, we understand summer has passed. Slowly, the anticipation of the hunt begins. Ventures afield involve poking around for tracks, trails, and other signs of deer activity. Memories from the past bubble up while wandering through the thicket. Even songs in their intrusive manner may conjure times past. They may be totally inappropriate for the moment, but latch onto the consciousness nevertheless. Being prone to lapses of attention while sitting in a blind or stand, I have begun a comprehensive analysis of songs and their relation to the hunt. If you are under a certain age, these titles may have little significance for you. Go back to texting on your smart phones. For seasoned outdoorsmen and women, here are some tunes that may just enhance the mystique of that Wisconsin ritual known as the deer hunt.

Mission Impossible.........What you are basically setting yourself up for when you vow to pass on anything besides a trophy buck.

Whiskey River......not so much a place, but a state of mind you will invariably reach at some point during deer camp. It might happen after that crucial missed shot, or during a late night game of cards, but it is inevitable.

Sherry, Sherry Baby........a type of beverage you realize you should not have mixed with the above-named river, even though it is a camp tradition. This realization hits about the time you need to be up early and on your stand.

Have You Ever Seen the Rain......Usually, you will ponder this question while sitting in misery on a morning you were fool enough to venture out in. Those weather anchors warned you last night, but they are always wrong, right? Oh yes, you have seen the rain before, but not quite this bad at a temperature one degree above freezing.

Nowhere Man.....the exact place you will inhabit when you discover everyone in camp has a deer on the meat pole except you!

Imagine......What you mainly do while sitting bored on your stand. That squirrel sound is a big buck moving towards you. A puffed-up "possum scratching in the leaves might be the trophy of a lifetime. You imagine you can tolerate the cold about another ten minutes before all circulation comes to a halt. That jerky you are gnawing on is the best steak in all the land. You wonder, could this type of hunt be had in Florida?

Good Vibrations.......This is a nerve-jangling sensation you will feel one windy day when your butt is planted in a stand you decided to place in a tree about six inches in diameter just because it was near a hot scrape. As vertigo takes its grip on your cranium, try to pretend you are being rocked to sleep by your lovin' mamma and you are diggin' the whole experience.

Bad Moon Rising.......The moon you encounter as the DNR warden shows up unexpectedly as you tune in your laser sights and night vision scope long after legal shooting hours. I suppose you could convince the authorities you were coon hunting with that AR15, but that is one tough trigger to pull.

Sounds of Silence.......Something you are not likely to hear over the snoring of you deer hunting buddies, Skeeter and One Bullet Bob. When you do fall asleep, it will most likely be amidst the unearthly quietude surrounding your deer stand, where even the rustling of squirrels has not been heard for days.

Sharp-Dressed Man......Precisely what you do NOT look like in your jungle boots,blaze orange aviator cap, and awkwardly - stuffed fanny pack you picked up at Farm and Fleet. Somehow that Doe in Heat spray dribbled onto your clothing as well, following you around like a tick on a dog and adding to your overall woman appeal.

Let it Be........What you should be thinking about that steamin' fresh road kill you are thinking of tagging just so you have something to show friends, family, and hundreds of motorists as you lash it to the hood and proudly drive it home.

On the Road Again.......what you will soon be after you get home and your wife and family get over the shock of that carcass on "their" car, your slovenly appearance, and musky odor. Better take a hot shower and quarantine yourself in the garage for a few days.

Olga Jurik and the Cold

JURIK HUNCHED OVER a steaming bowl of cabbage soup, watching a few tiny fat droplets jostling about the surface. Trancelike, he seemed to be probing a deeper reality within this microcosm of vegetables and bacon scraps. Breaking the early morning silence, his wife Olga stepped into the tiny cabin. With her came a flood of light and insect-like flecks of snow, which Jurik did not seem to acknowledge.

"I know Olga. It is time to bake the bread of winter. I have seen the snow even last night while you and the children slept."

"There will be enough for us, as always my husband. Even some strips of dried salmon have been saved."

` "I wonder if it is good to know this. Thinking of this fish might make it hard to sleep. We have never had much of this delicacy through the lotska. It seems almost wasteful to do this, when others have only bread. It is not part of the tradition."

"It will be good for us. The children worked hard for this extra blessing, smoking and drying all they could. There are some dried berries as well that I have not told them about. They are hidden well."

"Ha, we might as well fix our thoughts on jars of candies or coffee." Olga paused a bit, not quite sure how to respond.

" In my household as a girl, we ate such things through winter, but only tiny bits. They made me feel stronger and less achy in the spring. It will be fine. The clothing is ready, and no moths have been at it that I can see. There is plenty for all no matter how terrible the cold. We are lucky to have the children to help out. They awaken more easily. I used to worry that I might not wake up at all, but we always do."

Jurik nodded approvingly while picking at his teeth with a small splinter. He too used to fear the deep sleep of lotska. Now, it seemed more of a welcome respite from the endless toils of warmer days. Much like draft animals, he and Olga spent the warmer months hitched to the yoke of endless toil. Each had a role in knowing how to plod through the routine of each day. There was no need for much talk, especially complaints. This partnership was necessary to meet their meager needs. Regret was a concept alien to their thoughts. Jurik rose from his chair with a sigh, and ambled past his wife, giving her a gentle pat on her shoulder. Pausing at the doorway, he gripped the cold, stiff leather handle and gave the sturdy wooden barrier a slight tap with his foot. Outside, he surveyed the spires of coniferous trees that cradled his world. Through a distant clearing, he could not see the horizon through the light snow that had moved in like a fog. The snow was late this year, but he knew that soon his world would soon be buried many feet deep in it. The shovels that leaned against log walls looked to be in fine shape. Movements outdoors would soon be restricted to short burrows that had to be dug here and there. He turned and entered the cabin.

"We have some time, Olga. The real snows will hold for awhile."

"It will not be a long while. We must speak to the children to make sure they understand their chores each day, how each of us must take our turns keeping the fire." Jurik gave a short wave of his hand.

"They know. They know. Thankfully they are no longer little children. They handled things well last year. I am proud of them."

"Will we keep our own tradition and have a last special meal before we lie down together?:

"Do not tell them yet. I did save some dried caribou meat, and have a few sips of vodka your cousin gave us as a present." Olga's eyes brightened.

"Vodka?"

"Even a sip for each of the children. They are old enough. It will help with the sleep. So it is. We will rest again soon until the grass is seen to come up again. As does the bear, we will awaken as fuzzy-brained children, stumbling and weak. Our strength will return, and we will work again. Then will eat all we can and sing our traditional songs. Winter, like life, will pass quickly."

Turnip
Humble of the earth
Tasting of it
With butter, herbs, and cream
So far above it all.

Auld Danged Line

IT IS THAT time of year again to resolve to do better. Time to relax in the warmth of your home and go through all your outdoors belongings. Time to clean up a bit and organize. So, let's make two piles, things to cast out, and things to save. No use holding on to a bunch of stuff that just clutters up your world. Here is how my comprehensive system worked for me this year.

Inside the tackle box is a bird nest of snarled line. No use for that! A hook with a dried......appears to be a dried minnow on it. Tough little fellow to remove now. Wait, the cat might like it! Hang onto it. What the heck is in that Zip-loc bag? Hmmmm, it appears the Power Bait needs to be tightly sealed. Toss it.....or maybe not. Perhaps a little soaking in water will rehydrate those twister tails. Save pile, check!

Clothes will have to go through the wash. Better check those pockets. A couple of acorns......nice big ones. Might be cute for ornaments. There is something else rattling around in there. Jackpot! Three sticks of jerky. Feels petrified and smells a bit like that empty bottle of doe urine, but there is no shelf life on jerky. Ha ha.....some great snack food for the next Packers game. Tore up the camo pants pretty well on some barbed wire, but Suzy can stitch those right up. Whoa......here is an extra pair that went forgotten. Let's try these on. One leg in at a time, pull them up, button the waist. Wait a minute. These must have shrunk in the wash. Can't quite get things cinched up here. Although, this is the year you resolve to lose those extra twenty pounds, so better hang onto them.

Let's see. Ah yes, the freezer. What a mess! Here is an unlabeled package. Feels like, like, oh yeah, that roadkill you picked up three years ago. Looks like a bullsnake. Well, plenty of time now to skin it out and make that snazzy hat band. What does this package say? Deer........deer suet! 2008. That's a keeper. Been meaning to show the kids how frontier folk used to render fat to make their own soap. A meaningful lesson in history for sure. This is the real stuff kids need to know.

Finally, before taking the mud-boggin' truck to the car wash, it might pay to spruce up the interior a bit. A ten minute investigation into every nook and cranny reveals a treasure trove of items for the "save" box. Under the seat, a handful of reflective tacks and flagging tape, which allowed you once again to find your way in and out of the small woodlot you hunt. A couple of lucky turkey feathers you should have stuck in your cap. Might have gotten that spike buck you missed. Everything adds up. Five Jolly Ranchers, a glove without a mate, chapstick, two empty airline bottles of brandy, and half a roll of perfectly good toilet paper.

All told, this was a productive and enlightening adventure. Even more encouraging.....most of the stuff saved is perfectly useful. Quite a haul in fact. Reduce, reuse, recycle.....that is the way to go.

After the Shot

I HAVE HAD the privilege of befriending folks who, for most of their lives, did not have the contraptions that make life so easy for most of us. I am not talking about cell phones that talk, or dishwashers, or heated car seats. During the part of my life spent in Colorado, John Hill and his wife Jo were steadfast friends, and true pioneers. They had lived in a log cabin, still standing, and explained to me that the greatest achievements of technology included indoor plumbing and the toilet. My grandfather lived a good part of his years as a younger man in the same conditions. No electricity, no plumbing, no washing machine. One could not run to the store to buy fresh oranges or even lettuce for a salad. Food from the Plant Kingdom was stashed into a root cellar for as long as it would keep. Many greens, like cabbage, were stomped into kraut that would keep forever. Meats were common fare, and preserved by salting, drying and smoking.

Being a hunter and a small scale farmer, I do understand where real nourishment comes from. While I would not choose to live solely from the harvest from my garden and the surrounding and streams, I could. Of particular importance is clean, lean, healthy meat. Most of ours comes from venison these days. The hunt is still an experience I relish, but not the killing. It is a difficult thing to sit next to an animal whose life you have just taken, and thank its spirit for being a source of sustenance. Typically, one spends hours in the woods, every fiber of being alive attuned to the task at hand. It is meditative, and soul-cleansing. Red squirrels and nuthatches chatter away. Raucous bluejays squabble over anything and everything. All is in focus, and all is well with these creatures that have to endure the cold and harsh winters. I often wonder how they do it. They are tougher than we are, and embrace each day without remorse.

I hunt mostly with arrows, and getting close enough to an animal to look into its eyes is very different than dropping an animal with a gun. I marvel at their sleek perfection, and it is always a heavy decision to finish the hunt. After the shot, I often sit next to the deer, or grouse, or fish, and give pause for thanks.It is about as close as I get to prayer. Often, enveloped in darkness, I fully realize the profound nature of what just occurred. There is both satisfaction, and sadness. I suppose the best way to deal with this is always with a bit of meditation given to me from a Lakota spiritual leader many years ago, Selo Black Crow. I noticed when we ate, he would always take a small piece of meat and bury it, giving thanks to the "Great Mystery." I still feel it is appropriate to follow this with a special request to this same Creator.

"May my body someday feed the grasses that feed your kind." As things stand now, it surely will. Each molecule in us comes from something that has already existed, be it plant, animal, or mineral. These bits of matter do not die, they are simply recycled. I enjoy that thought, even after plucking some fresh green beans, that do not seem to mind at all.

Dreams are reality
Without consequences.

Thoughts While Fishing

Grasshopper on my hook
Consider your life and its end
Men have lived thusly
Hooked through the vitals
Repeatedly washed along the same currents

The hook is well set
Line strong and fresh
Unbreakable
I know your future
It is mine
You think your belly is being filled
That the day is going well!

Rainbow fish
As I spider you from your water life
I see that your eyes too
Are pleased by the aspen's lemon yellow streakings.

Kayaks......A New Geriatric Meter

HAD THERE BEEN someone present with a camera during my most recent outdoor outing, I am certain the segment would have gone viral on YouTube. It had nothing to do with a vicious battle against a musky. I did not single-handedly go head-to-head with a large boar armed only with a Bowie knife. No, I faced the daunting task of extricating my fat ass out of a miniature kayak.

Most would not view this as the equivalent of scaling Mount Everest. I suppose many would scoff at such effort as irrelevant. Maybe I have low T. I don't know. If you are over the age of 50 and tip the scale beyond the 200 mark, try this exercise. (You might wish to employ the efforts of a spotter.) Sit on the floor, legs straight out in front, and use your massive power of will to stand up. Did I forget to say one of the rules is you must do this without using your arms or hands?

It is said the first thing to go on a boxer is his legs. At age 60, I rely on my upper body to pull me out of the bathtub with one of those geriatric handles. Unfortunately, after a recent, successful crappie fishing trip, I began to wonder more and more about how to get out of my restrictive, floating coffin.

It was easy enough to get into the tiny flotation device. (I hesitate to call it a boat.) Gravity does most of the work, and a massive amount of butt-scooting will eventually get you and the craft launched and floating. After two hours of fun panfishing, the old legs were starting to cramp up. I wanted to stand and stretch, but it was out of the question. My kiddie kayak was a tippy little thing and not the kind you see guys fly fishing from on television. In spite of this, it carried a minnow bucket, a fly rod and spinning rod, a container of crawlers, and my tackle box. All of these remained wedged nicely between my legs. Accessing them was a feat in itself.

Finally, it was time to paddle to shore and remove my stiffened carcass from the plastic wedge. It seemed prudent to grab all items and toss them onto the shore, since I could not move at all with them in the kayak. Then came logistics. There was no pier to hang onto. Push on the left side of the boat, you capsize. Ditto for the right. I could not use my upper body. This was trouble indeed. The shallow water looked inviting on this hot day, and I was about to get wet. With a deft shoulder roll, I managed to get part of my aged torso into the shallows and slowly drag myself through the algae-laden wet sand onto the beach. I prayed nobody was watching this.

Finally, in a slow, grunting, grimacing fashion, I stood. What blessed relief! It took a few minutes of allowing blood to flow back into the right body parts, but I did regain equilibrium. I breathed a sigh of relief, loaded my gear into my truck, and turned the plastic chamber of horrors over to flush out the many minnows I dumped into it.

"Never again, little boat," I vowed. I eyed the nearby rowboat with envy. A few days later, my friend advised me I could have used the rowboat.

The Old Fisherman

He sat by the water's edge at night
grizzled, whiskered old stump
eyes caught for a moment
fastened to a galaxy of tiny fishes

Reaching beneath cold, sulking lily pads
net-like as hands
dabbler God scattering them in waves
chuckling, making merry with them
heart darting through the shadows of pond weed
dancer in the company of minnows.

Four limbs, a backbone
Craving oxygen
Weightless
We are all fish.

Orthoceras

YESTERDAY, I SAT in the stillness and humid heat of Muyil Mexico, on the steps and inside the doors of some Mayan ruins that are still being excavated. One cannot help but ponder the many feet that ran up these steep, treacherous steps and what they did when they reached the summit. There were no tourists here yet, just the sultry atmosphere of a jungle home much unchanged for thousands of years. A fine time to meditate until the mosquitoes get you up and moving.

Then, there exists another type of antiquity. It is far older, and its pages are measured not in years, but millions of years. This is the book of geologic time. Its every passage is measured by a clock that is incomprehensible in its age. Yet, the wonders of its contents remain intact and very legible. Its lessons are simple......change is a constant. Species appear, struggle for survival, and even the most successful may eventually disappear. Such is the world that Orthoceras thrived in for countless millions of years. I think of this world when I hold my fossil of this creature. One large landmass, Pangea, dominated the earth, a planet warm and full of shallow seas where it seems life exploded almost all at once. This was the steamy, wonderful incubator of all life in its manifold and glorious forms that would later populate our world.

It is well accepted that life, including the forebears of vertebrates, emerged from these early seas. Orthoceras was a creature related to modern-day squid and octopus. Like many of us, it was a hunter. It had a straight shell, much like an elongated ice cream cone with ridges. Like its relatives, it moved backwards by ejecting water under pressure. One can see the shell is divided into segments, and it is thought that some segments could retain floatation gases that allowed the animal to control its buoyancy. As it is with most animals, it was both hunter and hunted. Within the strata of rock in which it is found, there are trilobites, snail-like, spiraled ammonites, and countless other life forms that thrived on reefs in these shallow seas. What a spectacle it would have been to behold!

For those of us who spend our best moments in the outdoors, a keen understanding of the antiquity and ubiquity of life is essential. One of my former students, a successful civil engineer out west, took an acquaintance hunting for fossil shark teeth up high on a desert mesa. The man asked in disbelief how sharks could have ever lived up in this high desert. Go figure. Even though he had gone through school, he was never really educated in the way the natural world operates. To be ignorant of this is a travesty in education even today, when many still fear offending the erroneous tenets of some religions.

Orthoceras, along with trilobites and a wealth of other creatures went extinct, even though in their day they were among the most successful inhabitants of the planet. Continental plates shifted. Asteroid impacts devastated the planet from time to time. We as humans are not immune to, and even perpetrators of global disasters, though some would deny this. I love my fossil collection of life forms that predated the dinosaurs. I cannot comprehend the antiquity of these creatures, but revel still at the forms and symmetry that developed in that ancient world, laying the foundation for present-day plants and animals. Like looking at the immensity of the universe, it is humbling.

It Will Always be a Real Tree for Me

I HATED TO throw the scraggly brown thing out, considering what I had paid for it. It still seemed expensive, even though I waited until the last minute to purchase it at a discount. It was one of four trees left, a balsam fir, which I am partial to since the needles don't prick so much as they are decorated. These just happen to be the most expensive as well. Still, it is a luxury I refuse to give up. It has to be a real tree, with real sap that smells like the northwoods.

I have been told the smart thing to do would be to purchase an artificial tree. They are real dollar savers in the long run, and some look scarily realistic. You can even spray pine scent on them for an air of authenticity. They come with every manner of colored flocking and go up in a jiffy. They negate the trauma of killing a real tree. I hate them all! In my mind, they rank right up there with artificial wood stoves that get their "realism" from a red bulb reflecting off rotating foil.

Nope, there will never be an artificial tree in my home. I suspect this goes way back to childhood, when Dad came home lugging our tree. We kids helped with the precarious task of setting it upright in its holder, hands sticky with pitch and emanating that woodsy odor.

Even the cats would get excited, and always claimed their lair beneath lower branches. Ornaments and tinsel became instant toys.

Perhaps my best memory of a Christmas tree comes from a time when I was much too poor to afford one. I was a beginning teacher, and my Colorado rancher friends were always eager to help me, from allowing me to fish their stretches of a creek, to filling a deer tag. They never hesitated to allow me to cull a tree from their acreage. At the elevation where most humans lived there, around 7000 feet, there were no majestic, steeple-shaped spruce or fir. Gnarly pinyon pines and cedars presented the only opportunities. That was okay by me. After a short jaunt up the road in my beat up Jeep Wagoneer, I spotted a promising patch. This was about as good as it was going to get.

As I emerged from my old gas guzzler, and headed towards the tree of my choice, I noticed a bed of deer bedded peacefully beneath its boughs. A light snow was falling, and I just stood there and took in the moment. In time, the deer slowly moved off, and I headed up the slope.

I recall a moment of regret at having to take the life of this tree, as I still do. There is some consolation in acknowledging that this is some kind of honor for the tree. After the first bite of the saw, it all goes rather quickly. I recall this tree to be a specimen twisted like an oriental bonsai by the harsh environment it inhabited. It was indeed a bit odd looking, but it remains the most special tree in my memory. I wish I had taken a picture of it, but all that remains are the memories.

Is it not the meandering imperfections
In the grain of wood
That give it strength, beauty, and character?

Tree Stand

When I hear you
it will be as a rustle on dry oak leaves
or not at all
coming in, head down
with a heart more still than my own

As I fumble with life
miles above you
your step continues
precise, measured
testing the wind

I dream.....
not knowing whether we shall meet
in this darkness
feeling you out there
stirring briefly in the soft drizzle
that dampens your sea of corn.

Fourteen Months

HE WAS NOT a cat that immediately grabbed one's attention. Sitting on his carpeted perch, a bit aloof, amongst the more playful cats at the Clark County Shelter, he was by no meant a stand out. Being a retired teacher and cat lover, I decided to do my good deed for the world by doing a thing that comes naturally to me, and that is playing with felines. I relate to them a bit more than people, and at "Kitty City" I always felt good about the place and the fact it is a "no kill" shelter. It is actually quite a nice home for cats.

I found my former cat loved more than anything to play with a home-made mouse tied to a fishing line. Even in his last days, Squeaker would rally himself for the chase. Being without him lest a huge hole in my life. It was filled by a somewhat feral adopted girl named Daisy. She has a wild side to her, but is a wide-eyed, lovable sweetie of a cat. I wanted to adopt another, a mature cat that would perhaps not be high on a list of adoptees.

And so, I returned time and time again to play the "fishing mouse" game with all the cats in Kitty City. So many personalities. A few dominated that game, and hogged the mouse. Others would play when prompted. Given half a chance, I would have taken a mess of them home, but as for most folks, this was impractical.

Finally, I had settled on a few I thought would make good companions for our crazy, silly girl at home. I brought my wife Susan with me to help in the decision. Rather than the few I had singled out, a long-haired, squinty-eyed fur ball kept getting our attention. Not for playfulness, but just acting like a big ball of love that enjoyed petting on one's lap. A snuggler he was, who simply radiated an angelic nature. He had been given the name Dauber, which I was not fond of at first. Over time though, it seemed to fit. He was a big, innocent dabbler, dauber, whatever. We sometimes called him Daubner with the extra N, and Governor D.

So, one happy day in late August, we took him home. His stature and big feet were a stark contrast to fiery little Daisy. She did not take to him at first, but he made every attempt to be her friend. Soon, they became playmates of sorts, she being the faster, wild demon. He being the loping bubba who could somehow wrestle her to the ground if he caught up with her. Their "fights" were simply some kind of show of affection.

December 27 was a night like many others. The wood-burning fireplace was shut down and we went to bed. Susan brought in our chicken from the cold coop. She enjoyed the basement, gave us plenty of eggs, and was spoiled as chickens go. The cats viewed her as a constant source of amusement. I had gotten up several times during the middle of the night, and all seemed well. About 5:15 am, there came the sound of our chicken clucking, and the cats running all over the place. As this did not seem all that unusual, I rolled over in bed. Susan got up, and startled me by saying she thought something was on fire. I bolted from bed, ready to grab the extinguisher. I could see nothing. There was not a sign of fire anywhere. No alarms had gone off, but the animals were acting strangely.

Suddenly, Susan exclaimed "The house is on fire." An orange lick of flame shot out from above the deck, coming from the roof of the house. Then came a sickening, vibrating sound. The house reverberated. As I dialed 911, thick, black, toxic smoke came billowing in from the garage area. We bolted out the front door. It slammed behind us, and our world. I thought for a moment and grabbed a log from the porch and backed in the door, so the cats might have a chance. Small explosions and popping noises permeated the dusk. I had to move back, but could not leave. So long as there was a chance, I had to watch the door for those cats.

Clad only in boxer shorts, a T-shirt, and bare feet, I remember coiling into an almost fetal position, distraught in a wretched, sickening state of waiting, waiting, and knowing any help was going to be far too late. It was. Supplied with boots and a hat and coat, I at and watched the futile efforts to contain the fire. There was nothing left, Nothing, and I was convinced to go across the street to the ranch of Brad Krueger.

At some point, a fireman came in holding something beneath his coat. It was a charred and terrified little Daisy! The chicken, being the in basement neat sliding glass doors, had survived as well. My hopes were up that in some strange way, Dauber might be found as well. It did not turn out that way.

After a time, the eerie orange luminescence vanished from the sky, and the trucks and firefighters made their way home. I went back to sit there, watching, calling, and wondering if Dauber might have gotten out. He never did. After weeks of offering rewards, setting out food, checking tracks in the snow, I know he was gone.

Even now, months after the fire, when our house is now rebuilt, I feel his presence. I sit and wonder whether, had he known of his fate beforehand, would he have chosen to come with us. I believe he would have. We had him 14 months. In that time, the love he gave and received was beyond measure. I am haunted by these recent memories. In time, I know it will fade, and the pain will become less intense. I still think of him so often, and live in the spot where he perished. Such pure love we cannot expect from humans. Our girl Daisy has recovered, except for a tiny burned patch that grew back pure white on her flank. How she came from that twisted wreckage that melted everything, I have no idea. She ran to the basement, and I suspect Dauber ran upstairs, where he likely hid under the couch. That is all I know. That, and an inner assurance that, for the time we had him, he gave us all the love he had. He would not have traded those months for anything else.

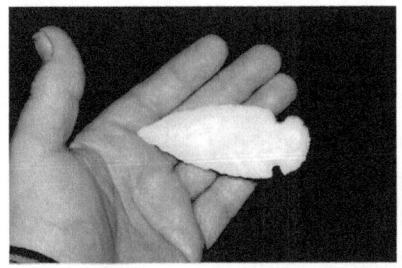

Arrowhead

I LOOK DOWN a lot as I walk. Hunting is an ongoing venture this way. Following a track, foraging for tasty wild plants, and of course scanning the ground for fossils and minerals specimens entails attention down there. Being a nearsighted kid, I could focus just fine on my feet for most of my life. When it came time to get reading glasses, bifocals were suggested. I tried to get used to this for an exceedingly short time until I discarded the idea. I suppose for city folk, walking on a level sidewalk and only looking down to read, bifocals can be quite utilitarian. Not for me. You have to know where you are placing your feet or you will suffer the consequences of a slippery root, a rock that someone dared to put out in the woods, or even a rattler napping under that log you just stepped over. Worse than this, you will never find anything looking straight ahead.

Having had the good fortune of being allowed to hunt a promising woodlot surround by corn and soybeans, I was being the diligent scout long before archery deer season began. Thanks in part to plows, areas that were once forest became fields. It was always exciting to discover areas of exposed rocks and pebbles, particularly if these contained flint and flint chips. After the winter or a good storm, the process of erosion revealed new possibilities.

One day, I hit pay dirt. Poking up from the dark Wisconsin soil was an arrowhead, complete as the day it was lost. It was not my first, nor would it be my last, but it was special to find it here on "my" hunting grounds near Walworth. I sat down and fondled it, cleaning off some dirt in the process. I wondered what the last hand to hold this point looked like, and who it belonged to. How different the terrain must have appeared hundreds or even thousands of years ago. While I could fantasize about our commonalities, it would have been impossible for the indigenous man to picture my world. Just down the road was a grocery store filled with goodies one did not have to stalk. It was cooled in the summer and warmed in the winter, and visited by members of my tribe in their shiny carriages, also with appropriate temperature controls. Motor boats scurried around Lake Geneva at speeds that he would not have understood.

Bright lights lit up the forest paths used by his tribe. Fearful thunderbirds spread their wings above, roaring overhead to places unknown.

His world would have been equally perplexing to me. Did he tough out the brutal winters here, or migrate to a warmer area? Was he living with a squaw and children? Was his home a teepee, or bark covered hut? While I could look up the answers to most things like this, I never did. It has always been a meditation for me to take that chiseled point into the hunting woods and to fondle it imagining my connection with its maker.

As tough as life must have been, my spirit friend probably had it better than many. The fertile soil and many streams feeding numerous lakes and wetlands afforded fishing, and vast beds of wild rice. I tried the freshwater clams only once, and that was not a good experience. Maple trees were tapped for their delicious syrup. Gardens of corn, squash, and beans were tended by the cowoman. I have eaten many of the seasonal treats they would have harvested here. Hickory nuts, certain acorns, and black walnuts grow in abundance. Berries like red mulberry, elderberries, and wild raspberries burst forth in warm months. Game animals proliferated in this abundance, and it is easy to see why tribes enjoyed relative prosperity in this region.

So, for all the trappings of civilized life, or should I say technological life, I doubt if my native friend would have traded up for all our conveniences. While I would give anything to be transported back to the time when my arrowhead was fashioned, I am not certain I would trade places for long. Still, it gives me great comfort to pause and contemplate the commonalities of our hearts. Our spirits still resonate to the same sights, sounds, and songs of the natural world. It is a world we do not own, but simply pass through.

To The Stone Giant

Another day beneath the sun for me
as men see only waves of heat
shimmer from my hulking, mammoth face
eyes fast upon lifeless shell
housing untamed, ancient spirits
whose hearts now beat as one with mine

Muffled chanting deep within
remains an echo intact
knowing that
if this thin green crust of life
feeding from its mother's back
should pass
it would leave only tiny, tiny scars.

Cold Day in Deersville

WE HAVE ALL been there this winter. Temperatures outside cold enough to freeze human skin in a short time. As I look out the window now, ghostly forms of icy shape shifters scatter across the barren cornfield, obliterating from sight most forms of life activity. Warm in my human den, I cannot help but contemplate the plight of the deer I hunted just a short time in the past. They are out there, yarded up somewhere, toughing it out.

I try to envision my survival in that deep freeze, with no warm bedding to crawl into at night, and I cannot fathom the depth of what I feel must be their misery. Or is it? After all, deer do not think like we do. They must accept and adapt to whatever Mother Nature throws their way. They have gotten good at this over the last million or so years. I too often picture myself in their situation. Would I approach some tree stand with a hunter in it and beg to be shot, knowing the misery that would soon blanket my forest home?

Thankfully, although I am certain deer can feel miserable, they carry on, without thought of tomorrow or yesterday. Just today. Adaptations they have for their stoic stance on life are incredible. I have often viewed their short coats and wondered how that skimpy covering could withstand the deep freezes of the north country. As it turns out, they can.

Deer hair in winter is composed of guard hairs that are hollow, trapping insulating air. Beneath is a finer, tangled undercoat. This combination is so effective, a deer can have snow on its back that will not melt from the body heat beneath. Kind of like a house with a well-insulated roof. Muscles at the base of each guard hair control their angle, fluffing up when necessary. Oily secretions keep all this very water repellant.

Beneath this effective coat is a layer of fat that is burned for fuel through the harsh months. The whitetail can turn down its metabolism by half in order to conserve this precious life sustaining stuff. The woody shreds of saplings they chew on are very low in nutrients, so the fat layer is critical. A deer can burn more calories seeking out woody browse than they get from the food itself. Even here, there is a strategy nature provides. Yarded deer seek sheltered areas, often under tall pines and other conifers, where the snow is less deep. Plowing through snow burns a tremendous amount of valuable energy. You have been there and done that. When it is necessary to move, the deer forge trails they use over and over. There is no need to barge through several feet of snow after the trails are initially laid down, and followed rigorously. The non-nutritious bits of food that can be had are helped through digestion as microbes in the deer's gut change from their summer composition, to a population that can better break down woody matter.

It is known that, as one travels from south to north, the average size of deer get larger. This is true with many mammals. (No disrespect to my fellow Wisconsinites.) The larger size gives less surface area to body mass ratios for these winter-ready creatures. The result, of course, is less heat loss.

So, while I dress in my layers of thermal underwear, alpaca socks, hat, and insulated jacket, my sleek fellow woodland inhabitants are no doubt much warmer and less jangled by the weather than me. They will lose their extra weight, while I struggle to maintain. They will have more camaraderie, less anxiety, and fret less about tomorrow than I will. Still, I will not be trading places any time in the near future.

Desire

I NEVER THOUGHT I would write this. Perhaps the time has come. Each year I age, there is a fear that bubbles up inside. It is of those things you do not think of in your youth, but now, it haunts me. It is the nagging thought that, some day, the desire to hunt will disappear. I will admit to being a hypochondriac, running to my doctor with every hangnail, tick bite, and paranoid fantasy. I am assured I am fine, and that keeps me that way until, in the middle of some night, I begin to doubt.

All my good friends hunt, fish, and relish the outdoors. In our talks, I have noticed a trend, which I vehemently deny, but one which permeates my soul. It is a question. The question is, will my passion to hunt ever die. I am certain that sounds absolutely silly coming from an outdoor writer, but it torments me. It is a form of impotence that I, as a man, do not want to confront. But I must.

I have run into so many men who at one time, were avid and enthusiastic hunters. Now, they hunt no more. Most are able to do so, yet have relinquished the tradition to a younger, more vibrant generation. I do recall the primal thrill of writhing in bed the night before a quail hunt, or field trial. The thrill resonated through every fiber of my being. Now, as a 63 year old man, I still succumb to waves of desire for the hunt, but they are not as intense. I have spent far too many hours taking pictures of fawns I find on my place, watching them grow, and yes the Bambi syndrome whacks me across the face at times. I can still arrow my neighbor's deer, just not "mine."

I have had the conversations with my soul. I can justify anything. If I don't harvest them, somebody else will. "Nature, red in tooth and claw" has no mercy for the young, the disabled, the old and weak. There is no easy death or natural death in the wild. How much better a quick end with so little suffering. I would wish the same for myself.

As most hunters agree, the kill is simply a culmination of inevitable circumstances. There is anticipation, the scouting and setup of a stand. The quietude of the pre-dawn darkness and evening dusk. the soft mossy trails festooned with edible mushrooms, the slick, widely spread hoof marks in the mud. Sometimes, the tiny ray of light piercing the black woods to follow a blood trail is a heady experience. Still, some intangible drive seems to wane.

No longer do I hunt much in the early morning. If it is really cold, forget it. I cannot swing from the tenuous branches and perch myself as I used to. Cushy box blinds and comfy seats rule my stand options these days. I love the fresh air, stealthy walks, and the total concentration of the hunt. Like many experiences, sometimes the satisfaction is in the journey, and not final shot.

> Life is our spirit's chance
> To live with animal passions
> And the curse of feeling guilt for them.

The Lights

Theirs is a higher beauty
without form, incorruptible
spirits perfect
Resonating to energies alien
but to those few
Who, with them hear leaves change
and guide the fishes
staggered by waterborne odors
unable to find their birth streams

They will not let it go
remaining always
bedded with the deer
or snug up against some raven
watchful of home.

Channing

THIS IS A story about a side trip in my life, one into the past, and integral to the roots of my own hunting and fishing lifestyle. It involves a woman named Olga Miller. As a young man, my Grandfather Murawska lived in a log cabin just outside of Channing, Mich. It was not much, but it allowed him to work the railroad job he had, and be in a land full of game and fish.

Throughout my life, I had heard of the woman named Olga, and was never quite sure who she was. As a boy, it really didn't make much difference to me. However, as an adult now in my 50s, I am a bit more inclined to gaze into the past that brought me where I am at now in life.

I recently had a unique opportunity to talk with Olga Miller's daughter, Jeanette Lindemann. I was in Eagle River, and Channing looked like just a short drive on the map. My wife wanted to spend some time organizing the cottage, so I had no excuse not to meet the lady that was able to tell me so much about my family history. She still lives in Channing, just a stone's throw from where my grandfather's cabin once stood on the Miller farm. I really wanted to see this spot, and learn more about the adventurous times spent there by my family.

I could not quite find the place, so I went to the only store in "town" and asked. After correcting my pronunciation of the name, I was directed to a house on Turner Road that is quite recognizable and "has all the really nice flowers in the garden."

I knew this woman was well into her 80s, but would not have guessed it by her high level of energy and enthusiastic welcome. There seemed to be some immediate connection. Jeanette brought out some cheese and crackers to snack on while we dug through old scrapbooks. There seemed to be a story be hind each picture, some of them of my grand-father, and my own father when he visited there as a child. The photos of her husband Johnny Lindemann, were portraits of a tall, lanky man with a definite twinge of mischievousness in his demeanor.

Being almost 10 years older than my father and an outdoorsman of local repute, he became an instant hero in the eyes of my dad. They got on splendidly and became good buddies. He took my father out to his secret spots on rivers and streams fished by Hemingway, and the nearby Michigamme reservoir.

Jeanette told of the wild nature of the place. A small set of deer ant-lers on the wall was the result of some boys goading her into shoot-ing a deer. It seems in those days, game laws were rather liberally interpreted and seasons did not mean all that much. In fact, Johnny's reputation as a crack shot was based in part on the fact that he could sit on the hood of a car moving through backwoods roads and pick off grouse with a .22 while the car was in motion.

There in another photo was a slim, attractive woman sitting with a bear propped up on her lap. It had been trapped and it was her job to dispatch it, armed with only a .22!

Another incident recounted involved her husband being caught in a trap set underwater to drown beavers once the trap was sprung. Through some mistake, Johnny got his own hand caught in this set and it was pulling him under. He was screaming to Jeanette for some kind of help, and she jokingly replied with some quip about not wanting to get all muddy. As I understand it, after a string of profanity, he was finally extricated.

The production of moonshine was quite the cottage industry for a while in those parts and innocent-looking women were sometimes unknowing carriers of this cargo in their car trunks. In disputes over this trafficking, sometimes men were beaten up. She remembered a time when, as a child, they had to walk through the snow from their home to the railroad station a few blocks away to get help for someone who was bleeding badly.

In several pictures, my father and two uncles could be seen feeding a young fawn. The mother had been killed and Johnny felt compelled to bring it home to raise it. It became tame enough to have the run of the house, even bringing a doe to the edge of the yard one day when it had matured enough to become interested in such pursuits.

After my grandmother died, my grandfather and Olga kept in touch. The entire families made trips back and forth between Channing and Chicago. I will never know exactly what the relationship between these two was, but Jeanette told me that, at one point, my grandfather offered her mother a diamond. They never married, but kept in touch through the years.

In Jeanette's garden, I noticed some beautiful peonies. Since my grandfather at one point became a leading hybridizer of these flowers, I asked about them. They were indeed a gift from him, still splendid after all these years.

In the back yard, a tree full of bright-red sour cherries was in full fruition. I then remembered the tree in my grandfather's back yard of the same type. As a child on a swing attached to its branches, I gorged on the tart fruits I so loved. As we filled a bag for my trip home, I wondered if perhaps there was a connection here as well. I saved the pits from these cherries, and intend to plant them. Perhaps some day, my grandchildren will get a chance to enjoy these living ties to our family, and roots that sink so far back through time.

Grandpa on right

Outdoorsperson?

SOME WORDS JUST give me problems. Using them in my ramblings about the outdoors often has me scratching my head. Fisherman is one of them. One cannot refer to all humans who entice fish to their baits as fishermen. That leaves out the ladies and kids. But gosh darn, fisherwoman just does not sound right. What about the kids? Would fisherkinder be appropriate? I don't think so. I am afraid I am stuck using the term "angler" because "fisherperson" simply does not cut it either. Maybe fisher would work, except that could be confused a large member of the weasel family. Doesn't hunter work for hunters, skier for skiers, archer for those who hunt with bow and arrow?

This is not a matter of political correctness. Don't even get me going on that subject. Suspect used to fine before "person of interest" became all the rage. In school, little Bobby may have made a "poor choice" today. He speared a classmate in the arm with a pointy pencil. No, Bobby screwed up to put it a bit more bluntly.

I run into the same conundrum with the word "outdoorsman." In fact, all the terms I encounter in my handy thesaurus are no help at all. An outdoorsman is not precisely the same as a naturalist, environmentalist, or survivalist, so I have to cast these by the wayside. I know "outdoorswoman" is used, but it just does not sound right. Boonie babe is probably offensive to some, I am not sure why, but it has a better ring to it.

There are plenty more terms and phrases that stick in my craw. While my verbal tool kit is by no means all-encompassing, here are a few quips that just floor me. At times, my only response is thinly-veiled sarcasm.

> "Did you catch any pheasants on your hunt?"
> "No, I am not quite as limber as I used to be, and never could fly."
>
> "May I ask you a question?"
> "You just did. Now be quiet, I am trying to catch a fish."
>
> "Did you physically drag that monster buck by yourself?"
> "Physically, no. I accomplished the feat through a process involving mental levitation."
> "You mean you caught that fish just to let it go?"

That is from my Mom, bless her heart. I don't even try to answer that one anymore.

Would you like to know the honest truth? (Who would want the dishonest truth.) Using the plural of fish dumbfounds plenty of folks. If you are talking about a bucket full of one species, you can say "fish" for the plural. However, if you have mixed panfish in the bucket, it is a bucket of "fishes." Go figure.

Let us not forget terms used by some outdoors-loving folks that are just plain wrong. I once had a fellow come to the door with a scraggly, smelly, roadkill coyote skin. He then informed me he had just "skun" it and wanted to know if I could turn it into a rug. Okay, swam, swam, swum is fine English. Skin, skinned, and scun will not cut the mustard. Being a taxidermist, I often get asked whether a trophy fish can be "taxidermied." Sure. Just don't ask me to stuff it. I can carve and sculpt an anatomically correct form to mount the trophy on, but I only use stuffing in turkeys, usually for Thanksgiving.

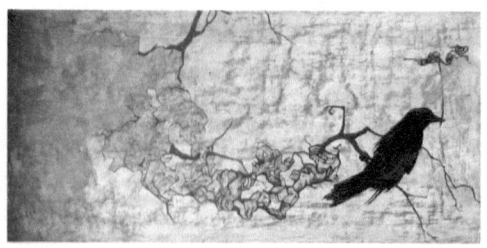

Talisman

WE WHO HUNT, fish, and forage are afflicted. Not just with the search, but with superstitions. Admit it. Talismans, amulets, charmed hats, lucky lures......we all sport them. Best in most cases if these ritualistic behaviors are kept to ourselves, or discussed only with a favorite shaman.

"Don't look that big buck in the eyes, they can feel it." Okay, sure, but only if it can see or smell me, right? (Chances are, it can.)

"Moss only grows on the north side of trees." I beg to differ. Look closely.

"Big lure, big fish." Hmmmmmm.......I believe some giant musky have been caught on minnows intended for crappie or walleye.

We have all heard the stories about the hazing that can go on in deer camps. Get a chunk of the heart from the first deer you shoot, and eat a raw bite. Now you are one of the tribe! Of course, in general, there is nothing better than carrying some jerky made from last years's deer into the woods with you on opening day. What could be better karma?

I will tell you what! I just ate a chunk of wooly mammoth. That is correct. Mammoth. Call it primitive, call it Neanderthal behavior, I just did it. What more power juice could a hunter get than from the ultimate prey? Folks in the Orient have the despicable habit of eating powdered rhino horn. Ditto for bear gall bladders and deer horn. Makes them real honchos. No so. This is illegal and for good reason. Rhinos are on the verge of extinction. Wild members of the deer family should not be poached for horn material either, although legally raised animals can be utilized for meat, horn, and hide.

Such piddly poo. I am talking about a giant, wooly mammoth. Taking that into my body must indeed confer upon me some mystic link with my paleolithic ancestors, right? Heck, I expect if I repeat this before each hunt, I might as well be invisible to the sensory apparatus of any creature, and my shots will all be dead on. Keep the scent blockers, grunt calls, deer pee, whatever. I now have the ultimate mojo.

Being a carver of gems for a hobby, I have always been fascinated by the trade in mammoth ivory. It is hunted for mostly in Siberia, where spring rains flood river banks, and wash out bones, tusks, and teeth from the permafrost. At times, mummified corpses are found, and sled dogs have taken hunks from the meat. I presume people have too. Not having been one of the lucky few to gnaw on some ancient jerky, I settled for the tusk. In the carving of my ivory, I had to remove pieces here and there. So, to take this sacrament into my spiritual realm, I filed off some rough edges and saved the shavings.

It was these shavings that went down the hatch with a chaser of sorts.

So now, I have taken one more step towards fighting osteoporosis, and nudged an inch closer to the loony bin. It is just me, or am I indeed feeling a bit more powerful, my senses keener, my wits sharper? I am not certain, but can proclaim with certainty, "I ate a mammoth."

Wolves: Not my Enemies

I AM SICK. Sick to death of seeing snippets of news, bumper stickers, and other avenues of communication damning wolves. In my area of Wisconsin, wolves have been on the increase. One poor soul at least was killed when he hit one on a motorcycle. Bear dogs free to roam the woods have been killed as they invaded a pack's territory. Deer and other game animals are supposedly ravaged by these incarnations of our worst nightmares. Wolves.

Living and hunting in this region, I have on occasion seen wild wolves. They appear to me to be sleek, beautiful, and amazingly fast creatures. I feel humbled to share the woods with these magnificent predators, who have been on the hunt longer than you, me, your daddy, or any relative you may have had a few thousand years down the road.

These social canines are the direct ancestors of the dogs we dote on and admire. Yet, they continue to be scorned. It seems top predators compete with the wants of man, and for that, they all suffer. To our prehistoric ancestors, competition with top predators was a serious thing. Today, it just raises the hackles of hunters who feel it is their God-given right to kill more deer. Wolves are not real competition to survival anymore. They can only interfere with our recreational pursuits.

I have seen the you-tube photos of wolf kills. Label them cruel. It is only a silly, anthropomorphic projection of what WE, the supreme predators, scavengers, and omnivores on the planet consider lopsided odds at hunting. Sadly, I have seen more pathetic deer road kills from autos than from wolves. I am certain more deer are killed on the road by cars than by wolves. Perhaps we should all stop driving. And yes, more folks are killed in deer/car collisions than from the big bad wolf.

What I think is most bothersome to the redneck mentality of "bad wolf" is the fact that they are too much like us. Just a wild guess, but I know for a fact we kill more deer, turkey, and other animals than do wolves. If they take some livestock now and then, oh well, let's contemplate Burger King and MacDonalds. As top predators, we do not like competition, unless it is sanctioned by us.

Ironically, we honor their descendants, aka dogs, that bend to our will and have provided us with so much since prehistoric times. How schizoid we are to admonish wolves for doing what we have encouraged our dogs to do so well..... to hunt and kill. How many breeds of canines have been named for the creatures they were bred to attack? Wolfhound? Foxhound? Rat terrier? Let us not forget that feral dogs wantonly kill livestock and wildlife for the sheer joy of it. I have seen it done to sheep, and it is a disgusting scene. I do not worry about wolf attacks in the woods where I hunt, but I do carry pepper spray and a gun for psycho dogs living in the suburbs, with mindless owners who could care less if they attack bunnies or bikers.

It seems we just cannot stop playing God. We now "manage" wildlife, forests, and all the things dear to us. Most folks who really understand nature value the role of predators in keeping populations healthy and normal. If that means I see less deer this year, and the ones I do see will be a bit less tame, I can live with that. Success is no longer measured in how many tags are filled, how many clueless deer pass under my stand, or how full the old freezer is. I sleep better knowing the predators are nearby, living and prospering in the same pine studded bluffs we both love to roam.

To Those Who Listened
To Us Making Love

They could have heard us
Those frogs floating in the swamp
Lobeless ears vibrating like drumheads
They would not understand
Although I have seen them grasp each other
In that way frogs do
Mindless of the other's presence

Others, the deer, listened without knowing
Ears cupped unerringly towards sounds
Vaguely familiar in a season of autumn passion
Memories unable to hold it

Only the coyote knew
Pacing a fence line, he stopped cold
Barked once and whirled around
In that moment, hunger left him
As he pawed the ground, turned tail
And ran into the night.

The Only Insurance

WE ALL PAY for it, at least most of us. There is some intrinsic comfort in the knowledge that, if I shoot myself in the foot, snag the back of my head with a musky lure, or fillet my left thumb, there will be some compensation through insurance. At times, it seems like a form of extortion, but let's face it, we all need it.

As outdoors folks, we collect a lot of stuff, useful and otherwise. We grow attached to these things related to our passions. Guns, fishing rods, lures passed from father to son through the ages retain a worth beyond measure. Such stuff appreciates in value as the years roll by. It is comforting to hold and use as a portal to other times, places, and memories. I often held Grandpa's gun, an intricately engraved double barrel 12 gauge that once belonged to a rough-hewn railroad man. To see it, you might expect the owner was an English gentleman, a dandy with a gun so beautiful, one almost dared not shoot it. I even had a patch of camo cloth cut from a pair of pants I had worn hunting for at least 15 years. I had to throw out the pants, but retained that one scrap for my "medicine pouch" of useless but precious memorabilia.

Naively, I assumed these precious acquisitions would follow me through all my years. I was wrong. A fire ended this dream as the pre-dawn darkness turned to light, and I watched our home burn to the ground. Every last piece of it. I stood with bare feet in the snow, too much in shock to want to move or leave the place I had collected my life in. I suppose I would have been okay with just lying down forever right there, with a beloved cat that never made it out. I was told we were lucky. Our chicken woke us. No alarms sounded as the upper roof burned. Nothing but the chicken.

It has been 5 months since that day. The insurance company has been wonderful in allowing us to rebuild, refurbish, and try to put this horror behind us. While stuff gets replaced, Grandpa's gun, photos of bygone times, fishing and hunting trophies, and memorabilia precious and known only to myself are gone. I was told shopping for new items would be fun. There is no fun in it. I will have "stuff" again, but it is not truly mine, and was not handed down to me with pride from generations past. That wood duck on the mantlepiece exploding from a duckweed covered slough will not be duplicated. The wooden decoys carved by friends cannot be substituted for. The holster I wore for many years of my life in Colorado cannot be purchased at in any store. Even if it could, it would not be mine.

Like photographs, I believe objects carry with them energies from the lifetimes they have shared with me. I now think should have placed them in a fireproof safe. Pictures could have been backed up and placed in a safe deposit box. We never believe a tragedy like this can so fully destroy what we cherish.

It cannot. So long as I can still envision my first trout pulled from a pond in Illinois, and relive every fall morning full of game birds exploding from the hedgerows over masterful pointers, there is no real destruction. As with hunting partners that have passed on, be they human or animal, their essence remains strong within. As ephemeral as dimly-remembered sounds, smells, and tastes.....the most irreplaceable memories will always remain very much alive. They outlive the most faded photographs. They outlast all of the treasured fishing rods, guns, and tackle boxes full of lures. The motionless trophy buck on the wall stares down no more. It now sneaks under a gap in the barbed wire fence as it did the day my arrow found its mark. That gape-jawed bass is freed from its driftwood pedestal on the wall, and skulks through lily pads and coontail as I remember it. While I have lost pictures of the pointing dogs that enhanced each hunt for gaudy pheasants and explosive quail, I can still feel them next to me, and smell their moist, dog-hair smell as I did when I slept with them in the back of our station wagon, on the long road home from the hunt.

Hope is a bright expectation
Faith is a hunch.

No Life Like Snow Life

I DON'T BELIEVE anyone in Wisconsin can argue that this last winter was a brute. Too much snow, too much cold, spring flooding. Who needs it, eh? Well, we do, as do the creatures who live here. Both game and non-game species benefit from some snowpack. While we can all bemoan the bad roads, and shoveling the white stuff, it is absolutely essential to preserve the health of many species. It provides a stable, insulated environment with lack of wind and high humidity. Take this away, and there is trouble for many. Plants and animals alike, including hibernating bears depend on this. Take it away, and some might say this was a blessing. It is not.

Some reptiles and amphibians can survive total freezing of their bodies. If a warm snap interrupts this death-like sleep, animals may reanimate, only to be decimated by fluctuating temperature drops. Prey species like voles and shrews rely on their tunnels under the snow for stability. Birds of prey that depend on these food resources will be impacted. I have seen grouse dive into snowbanks if they feel threatened, and it is a wondrous sight to behold. Deer are so well insulated that they can be covered with snow and it will not melt. It will insulate. In fact, Eskimos in icy igloos can start a fire inside and remain with only light clothing due to the insulating properties of snow. Even survival manuals tell how to build a snow enclosure for protection.

Some will argue that deep snow can make deer more vulnerable to predators. True enough. Wolves and coyotes love a crust on the snow over which they can easily run down hoofed mammals. Nature can be cruel, but it is not our place to try to improve it. Animals like the snowshoe hare and weasels turn white for camouflage in snowy environs. Take this away, and they stick out like a sore thumb.

Scientists call this zone of leaf litter and dirt under snow the sub-nivian zone. While temperatures above the snow might be thirty below zero, underneath it can be thirty two degrees or even above this freezing mark. Many small invertebrates which are food sources for larger forms of wildlife remain in this zone through winter. Ever see a large butterfly in March? It is probably a Mourning Cloak. The winged, adult forms of this insect seeks out cracks under bark and go into a state of cryo-preservation, only to emerge when they can catch the first warming rays of sun in early spring. Most likely the first butterflies you see each year. Dark with yellow margins on their wings.

Rabbits love a tall layer of snow. They can walk atop it and nibble at stems and twigs normally beyond their reach. Animals and plant life cannot be separated. Not only does a good snowpack give protection from wildfires, a slow spring melt is almost as good as drip irrigation for plants. Without snow, many plants freeze and just burn out. Of course, there is no ignoring some folks thrive on winter snow for sport. So, each year, don't cry and whine about it. Embrace it for what it is.......an integral part of Wisconsin and other northern ecosystems that is life-affirming and indispensable.

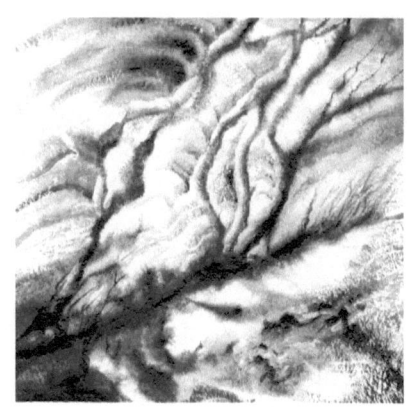

I Can Hear Crickets Beneath The Snow

In blue-white silence
Long - shadowed arms of sleeping friends
Point to seething stretch of frozen light
Where tingling ice children ceaselessly blow
Walk on
Hear the crickets beneath the snow

Brush away winter's dancing jewels
Above this cauldron of crystal cold
See beneath the hardened chill
A thousand yellow flowers below

And in this dancing golden glow
Reigns no somber silver pallor
To hide from green eyes
Windy blue skies
Sunbird's shimmering soaring days
Yesterday's sleeping summer past.

Fire is a Life All its Own

THE TIME OF cold is upon us. Few traditions evoke such feelings of comfort and camaraderie as huddling with friends and family around a crackling fire. In countless deer camps, fire will draw friends close together, and provide a perfect stage for the telling of tales. What soul can peer into the dancing flames and muse over a site that has mesmerized humankind since the dawn of time?

It strikes me at times that within the orange glow, life itself is being mimicked in a manner that can remind us of the stages of life we all pass through. Like ourselves, each fire starts off as a thought. We gather together bits of dead trees, who spent their lives soaking in solar energy and turning it into their tree substance. The time has come for these pieces to release that which once gave life to a majestic oak. As with all of nature, from death comes new life. The towering giant whose branches gave refuge to generations of birds, and its seeds to deer and squirrels, now gives back the last of its spirit.

As with our own birth, a tiny spark soon gives rise to a new "being." This entity mirrors many of the attributes of life itself. There is movement, warmth, and energy that grows. Like a child, it comes ablaze with all of its time still ahead. What was just moments ago just a flicker asserts itself with tongues of light, growing into a dancing whirl of crackling radiance. There is that initial bursting of energy we experience in our own youth, giving little thought to the future, embracing the vigor of the moment.

At some point, the fire reaches a kind of maturity. It no longer grows, and has left behind a trail of embers, which represent the past. As in life, they may be accomplishments, memories, or paths that never quite worked out. There is now a balance between what is and what has been, an equilibrium of sorts. It still burns with passion, radiating energy and a robust coming of age. As the fire shares this vitality with those clustered around, it seems it would be a good thing for it to remain in this state forever.

Yet, like ourselves, over time, the potency of the blaze mellows. Its pile of embers grows larger, and sustains what life there is to come. There reaches a point where, unless a log or two gets rattled around, no more new expansion can be expected. Life has a way of rattling us around like that. We flare again, then settle down, relying on the embers of memory to remind us that life has been worthwhile, and there are plenty here still glowing to remind us of that. In fact, those bright embers are now some of the best parts of the fire to stare into and contemplate.

Finally, the arms of flame no longer reach out for want of fuel. They are content to simply glow from within, while activity slows to an even pace. There is still plenty of life left in those embers, but the frantic activity of a conflagration is coming to a calm conclusion. With what energy they still possess, the luminous orbs can still ignite fire anew, as can elders we have revered in life. This is a turning point, when poking and prodding will no longer change things much. What has been accomplished or left undone is, for the most part over. There is no rekindling what has already been spent.

At last, some tiny chip of orange warmth will be the final one to disappear amid the bed of ashes surrounding it. Even now, the surroundings remain warm with the energy that has been spend during the life of the blaze. In time, they cool and are spread on the ground, once more part of the earth from which new life will spring. Once more they will enter a root, and become part of a molecule that absorbs sunlight, and live once again.

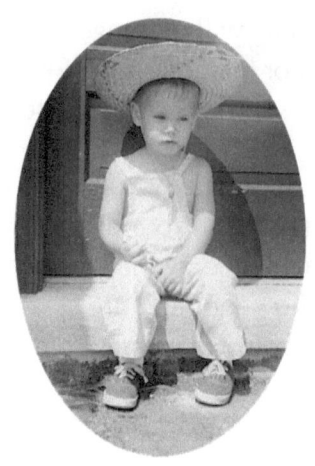

Aunt Mary's Corn

I HAVE HEARD it implied that tastes, smells, and sounds often linger in our memories beyond other details of life. I believe this to be true. Who can forget the smell of a new box of crayons, or the taste of a fresh strawberry? One of those recollections that has stayed with me a lifetime is that of an heirloom variety of corn, grown by my grandfather, known as Aunt Mary's sweet corn.

My first taste of this was as a pre-teen child, when I found great pleasure in sampling everything from Grandpa's verdant soil. He was a flower hybridizer of some of the most gorgeous iris and peonies, while at the same time being a cussing, tobacco-spitting, railroad man. Always in the local news for his 20+ pound cabbages and monster kohlrabis, it was his sweet corn that I remember most. Aunt Mary's is a pure white, non-hybridized plant. This means that each year, one can save a seed ear of corn, dry it out, and replant. This was done religiously. I have never tasted corn as good. He insisted it be eaten the same day it was picked or some sweetness would disappear. He was correct.

When my grandfather passed away, the traditions were no longer sustained. His garden was parceled into suburban lots, and has been gone for a long time. Still, in his house, my uncle Bill, who was a bit of a hoarder, kept things just as they were back in the early seventies. Nothing changed in the house, just the accumulation of dust and dirt. When Bill left this life, it was incumbent upon my folks to clean and tidy up the place for sale. In the process, an ear of Aunt Mary's sweet corn was turned up. Originally designated as a seed ear, it had lain in some forgotten corner of the basement for forty years. Could it be that there was still a spark of life in it that could germinate? Local farmers told me it was worth a try. Wrap some moist paper towels around the seed and watch for any germination.

From what I know about plants, this did not seem likely, but I was excited at the possibility that I could revive this magnificent strain of corn. I carefully plucked all kernels from the dried out cob, and packed moist towels around them. Others, I put directly into moist humus to see if sprouting would take place. Each day, I looked for any signs of life, but there were none forthcoming. The black humus simply molded over, and there was no sign of any germination. It was depressing.

In days gone by, there were many more varieties of garden plants than there are available today. Some farsighted individuals have preserved these, and many are available through the proper channels. As it turns out, a long internet search turned up the fact that, yes indeed, this heirloom variety is still being saved from extinction.

For this year, it it too late to plant, but next year, there will be a substantial parcel of my garden reserved for this corn. I will once again savor the taste and aroma of a treat not enjoyed for over forty years. I know it will take me back in time to a place in my memory that is forever special. New crayons, Christmas trees, piles of hay, and fresh sweet corn cannot be forgotten. I cannot wait for the trip to these bygone times.

Grandpa

IN THE OLD, sepia photo, he stands looking at me from a time I will never know. There are so many stories I could write about him. Born at the turn of the last century, as a child, he hopped a train and went to live with the Lakota Sioux on a reservation, at a time when some still talked about Custer's defeat at the Little Bighorn. They had been there. At one point, he decided to return home after he took a bath. Lice had been bothering him for some time, and he had grown tired of that.

His early years were spent in a log cabin near Channing Michigan where he lived off the land. I will tell more of that in another story.

I knew him only in his later years when he worked his garden that took up two city blocks. He never made it through high school, and played the role of a stubborn, curbing railroad man much of the time. Yet, his gnarled hands brought forth some of the most revered iris and peonies that garnered awards from Germany, the United States, and a letter from the royal family in England. He was friends with Myrtle Walgreen and was almost booted off the property by a butler when he showed up with some flowers. As always, he was dressed in his soil-covered railroad coveralls and must have looked out of place. He never cared.

This man was my grandfather. To each of his three sons, he passed on his prowess at hunting and fishing. Passion for the outdoors was a given in our family. Even before I could walk much of a distance, my father carried me on his shoulders like a draft horse through the fields near our home. It was there I first thrilled to seeing our pointers lock onto a pheasant, anticipating the explosive rush of wingbeats and the calking of a rooster launching itself into the air. I assumed everyone lived thusly, and fully understood what all the excitement was about.

From my grandfather, through my dad, to me came something that has steered my life from its onset. If I were a hunting dog, this might be explained in terms of bloodlines. Yet, there was as much nurture as nature involved in building my passion for the outdoors.

As a youngster, I earned much of my vast income by pulling weeds in Grandpa's gardens. So did most of the neighbor kids. We viewed him with awe and a perhaps a bit of fear. Here was a man who could still carry a deer on his shoulders at age seventy. We have the movies. Like most railroad men of the time, he chewed tobacco and introduced me and my friends to the heady experience of Copenhagen snuff at far too tender an age. He loved to feed squirrels as he sat on a picnic bench pruning flower rootstocks for sale. They would sit on his lap and even go into his house for treats.

From his gardens came twenty pound "atomic" cabbages as he called them, and radishes the size of a man's fist. He was a true green thumb, and folks came from all over the world to view and purchase the hybrid flowers he developed.

Grandpa walked the fields with his sons, and grandson until he could walk no more. The pure black pheasant he shot on one of these hunts still hangs on my wall. Nowadays, I still use his guns to hunt game birds and deer. My own father and uncle are now reaching an age when trekking the fields is becoming increasingly difficult for them. We still talk plenty about the old days, when quail and pheasants were more abundant, and there was more prime cover to hunt. Days when the hedge rows and brambles were always gnarlier, and osage oranges made for great shotgun targets.

I wish in some way I could pass my love of nature onto every child, as it was for me. As a science teacher, I try. Yet, the classroom is no substitute for being brought up in a family where so much revolved around the sights, sounds, and smells of the outdoors. For too many kids, the idea of gathering food from the wild is viewed as weird or gross. For these children, I feel sorry, for they may miss out on the better things in life.

Yet, every once in awhile, kids will come talk to me about how neat it was to be out in a duck blind before sunrise, or thrill to the tug of an unseen fish. I know that behind most of these encounters is a family member who takes time to nurture those things that make time spent in the wilds and ever sought after joy.

A Tribute to Treestands:
The Old and Forgotten

PRE-SEASON SCOUTING. NOW here is a subject that has been beaten to death by writers over and over again. I am guilty of not having spent my many seasons of hunting whitetail rigorously haunting the woods and fields in search of that perfect spot to place a permanent stand. Rather, I have often allowed hunters of days gone by to silently point out where to stake my claim.

Regardless of the time of year, finding an old stand fills me with the kind of nostalgia one experiences when looking at an old, dilapidated barn or abandoned home starkly silhouetted against the horizon. It causes me to pause and take in the spirit of the place. Who was the person that hunted here? Why this spot? Is the hunter still alive, or passed on? The feeling can, at times, be eerie. In the fading light, it is not difficult to imagine a ghostly form sitting watchfully in the dilapidated structure, surveying the woods below for the slightest twitch of an ear or tail. In my mind's eye, the spirit hunter chuckles to himself from time to time at the spiraling of squirrels chattering while pursuing each other around a tree trunk, and admiring the colorful bluejays as they gather acorns and alert others with raucous calls.

Whatever the case may be, I am not so very far removed from my ephemeral vision. Our goals were the same. Times were different, I suspect better in many ways, but here we pause, in some lucid dream connecting past and present. Some of the ancient stands still show a degree of sound craftsmanship. Others remain a mere couple of two-by-fours hanging by the rusted remnants of nails. Some are so precarious, I wonder how anyone got up into them, let alone sat on with any degree of comfort or safety.

I have been musing about putting together a calendar of iconic, old stands for those souls who, like me, pause in some reverence to the faded splendor of these artifacts. I have seen similar yearly planners put together with photos of old barns, covered bridges, and other vestiges of your past and heritage. I would love to edit such a production, and share the special spots that might resonate with this story. Please, feel free to connect with me, (I do not say "reach out") for I am an older guy. This year, be sure to pay homage to the ghosts of tree stands past.

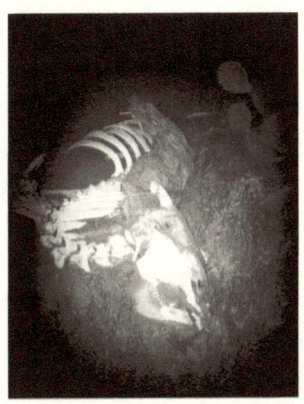

Stump O' Death

THE NEED TO decorate the outdoors in the form of artificial creatures has always given me pause for thought. They can range in style from very lifelike deer, birds, and bears to gaudy giant butterflies that glisten in the sun. I am not certain why folks put faces on trees, trolls in the trellis, or those silhouettes of Gramps bending over "gardening" with his rear sticking out.

While some of these can be realistic enough to act as decoys for their genuine counterparts, others are totally tasteless and out of place. Perhaps the poster child for the ridiculous are pink plastic flamingoes in Wisconsin. Others can serve a purpose, like an owl scaring ravenous birds away from garden areas. A few are simply seen as whimsical or cute. My wife loves a somewhat lifelike giant frog which reclines on our porch. We once also had one of those mallard ducks whose wings spiral round and round in the wind. I have to admit a certain fondness for it.

Chainsaw sculptures are popular, particularly in the northern part of the state. Some of these are indeed tasteful pieces of art, and fit in well with log cabins in particular. Then, there are resourceful individuals that come up with their own unique brand of creativity. Last year I ran into one of these monuments to man's love of nature that remains truly unparalleled in my experience. Right now the snows are probably melting enough to reveal one of the most incomparable shrines to the Neanderthal spirit that still permeates our beings.

I got a hint of its existence one day while fishing with my cousin Mike (The Pike) Eyre near Eagle River Wisconsin. As we fished slip bobber rigs for stunted panfish, Mike hinted that our fishing partner, Keith Silzewski had a highly-developed knack for finding and collecting "stuff" from the surrounding woods. From what I could gather, his home was a veritable museum of unusual rocks, driftwood, animal bones, and rusted gizmos.

Prominent in his front yard was the venerable Stump O' Death.

"Stump O' Death," I blurted. "What kind of oddity is this?"

"It's hard to describe, Den. Keith masterminded this triumph of engineering years ago, and has grown bit by bit ever since."

"Do you think I could get a picture?" Mike rubbed his chin and mumbled something under his breath. As it turns out, it was another year before I got to behold this macabre shrine in the pines.

It turns out Keith has an unusual gift for finding odd things during his jaunts into the forest. Beneath and around a nice Buck shoulder mount in his living room are assembled rocks, gnarly pieces of branches, and ancient oars. Some perfectly round stones could have been used for games by primitive tribes. A jar stood nearby, full of puzzling objects. Upon closer inspection, it turns out they were reflective tacks used by hunters to find their way in and out of thickly wooded areas where they hunted. Since I am notorious for getting lost even in the smallest patches of timber, I shot Keith a look of dismay and shook my head. He chuckled. I could only wonder how many hours hunters had stumbled around in the dark cursing the prankster that stole their beacons to civilization.

The doors and walls of his outdoor sheds are livened up with rusted old farm implements and an odd assortment of thingamajigs whose former functions can only be guessed at.

Finally, it was time to make the short pilgrimage to the Stump O' Death! As I understood things, Keith once had a rotting useless stump in front of his home. Born a hunter, Keith has taken his fair share of bucks, turkeys, and other critters. Being a nostalgic kind of scrounger, Keith was always loath to throw out anything. It seems at some point in time, Keith began paying homage to the not-so-wily bucks he had harvested by nailing their heads to the stump and letting nature take its course. Some might call this a "European" mount. I would not go so far as to call this any form of taxidermy, but it evidently satisfied some primal urge to honor the spirits of the deer departed.

In time, other talismans appeared on and around the stump. Turkey wings, squirrel tails, and various other odd artifacts are interspersed among the skulls. Time and the elements have molded this tribute to the northwoods into a relic any Paleolithic man would hold in awe. Even in the slightest breeze, it seems to become almost a breathing, living entity. The final monument remains a unique temple that perhaps only a true Yooper can appreciate.....the Stump O' Death!

We are all sentenced to death
The price of life.

Camouflage

IN THE WORLD of nature, camouflage has to rank among the most important survival mechanisms ever evolved. Both a defensive form of hiding and an offensive tool for surprise attacks, many creatures would be hopelessly inept at continuing their species without its protective influence.

No matter how much time one spends outdoors, it is always astonishing to come across some creature you have never seen before hiding in plain view. Just the other day, I was staring at the kitchen wall and noticed an irregularity. It was not in the coloration of the paint, but in the contour of the wall itself. Curious, I investigated to find a soft, powdery white moth pressed flat up against the textured white surface. Did it "know" it was hidden there? I believe it did. I have seen this countless times in moths and spiders that seem to seek out just the right color scheme and texture to disappear into.

Other experts of subterfuge take this to a whole different level. The flounder is one of my hidden heroes. This flattened fish only needs to see its background, and the neural input activates chromatophores in its skin to match whatever background it is pressed against. The octopus also possesses this uncanny ability, and can alter its body outline as well to blend in with clumps of coral, algae and sponges on a reef.

In short, they can "think" themselves into the appropriate disguise.

On a basic level, it may simply be colors that blend with certain backgrounds. In red rock areas out west, grasshoppers have adapted to match the rusty reds of sandstone.

Look at most fish, and the belly is almost universally lighter than the back. It is a matter of blending in when seen from above as well as from below. As the deceptions become more advanced, patchwork patterns that break up an organism's outline come into play.

This is the basis for some of the clothing developed for soldiers. The ghillie suit not only breaks up coloration, its rag-tag outline of strips of burlap mimics vegetation so well, a person garbed in these suits merely needs to hunker down and "become" a shrub, hedgerow, or overgrown stump.

Some forms of camo have to be analyzed a bit to understand how they work. For instance, a boldly-patterned zebra hardly seems to blend into its savannah environment.

Yet, as the sun gets low in the sky, the alternating light and dark stripes seem to become one with the silhouettes of sky and tall grass on the horizon. Since this is prime hunting time for predators, the ruse can work. Mimicry is another form of deceptive coloration in which a harmless creature takes on the coloration of one that is best left alone. Many flies use bold black and yellow stripes to imitate bees or wasps.

Eyespots can frighten a would-be predator into thinking it may have encountered a larger, more dangerous quarry. Moths in particular use this to their advantage. Various fishes use them to divert the attention of attackers from their real eyes to a less vulnerable part of the body. Stripes aligned with genuine eyes often conceal the true location of these targets.

Stealth technology now permeates the war scene. It is not enough to be simply visually camouflaged. Warm objects that give off infrared radiation need to be hidden. Radar is a constant threat to pilots who can be "seen" by its invisible, far-reaching rays. Thus, the development of stealth air- craft, boats and other vehicles that can hide from the ever-present threat of this penetrating form of detection.

Not surprisingly, some animals have evolved means for coping with "animal radar." Bats and some other mammals can locate prey by bouncing ultrasonic waves off themselves much like radar. Some moths have the capability of sensing when they are being scanned, and resort to crazy aerial maneuvering to escape being eaten. Others can mimic the ultrasound scan made by the bat and thereby jam its form of radar. If all else fails, the moth will sometimes dive low to the ground to evade its attacker.

As hunters head into the woods each fall, many will be wearing some form of camouflage. What started out as a simple pattern found in Army surplus stores is now a multi-mil- lion-dollar enterprise. Each pattern claims its superiority.

Some are great for corn fields, others for rocky outcrops covered with patches of snow. The newer ones may be textured with leaves and other protuberances to break up the human outline.

My ranching friends used to rib me about this obsession with camouflage. Their advice? Put on a pair of overalls with a flannel shirt and just walk out into the field. The deer will then supposedly not mistake you for a stealthy hunter and ignore you. Don't laugh too much—I have seen it happen!

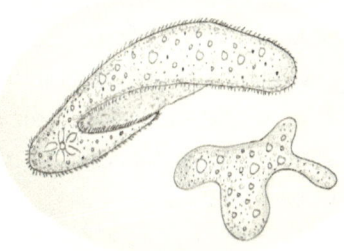

Starling

YEARS AGO, SOMETHING occurred that struck me as a revelation. It had to do with a certain bird that flew into the yard and perched on a nearby tree. I don't remember what I was doing at the time, but an almost urgent voice from my wife Susan urged me to come quickly and see something. This has happened on numerous instances. I hoped it would be something epic, like the time a black bear crawled up a tree next to our raised porch. As it turns out, the commotion was all over a "bird full of rainbow colors that was just beautiful, unbelievable!" It was a starling. Being close enough to see the iridescence radiating from the very ordinary visitor, it dawned on me that this bird was indeed a special sight to behold. It was not black. It reflected the full spectrum of color all about itself like some dark rainbow. To Susan, it was a spectacular discovery. For me, it became one as well. Seeing the childlike innocence of her excitement lit a spark in my own perception of the world.

We are all transfixed by the majesty of an eagle soaring above, and slam on the brakes to view a stately buck nibbling some twigs along the roadside. Yet, what we view as ordinary and mundane often never warrants a second glance. Dandelions splash the fields of spring with color, yet we disregard them as mere weeds. Moths press against the bark of trees and even the doors of our home, almost invisible in their perfect camouflage. Look closely. Before you is perfection. Often, they are swatted away without a second glance. We find so many things unworthy of the time it takes to learn their names and habits. It is a worthy endeavor to learn those names and identifying character-istics, and bid each form of life its' due.

I was fortunate to own a microscope from the time I was in sixth grade. It was a pretty good one. College had me peering through them all the time as a graduate student helping teach protozoology and parasitol-ogy. Every drop of pond water was like a trip to the zoo. There was the ubiquitous Paramecium cruising through a jungle of algae like a frenetic sprinter. As with many one-celled creatures, it has no eyes, brain, or nervous system at all. Yet, by bumping and backing up in its simplistic, hyperactive mode, it manages to fulfill all of its needs. This world, alien to most, is home to the the lovely pink Blepharisma. Like Paramecium, it cavorts through its watery world by means of tiny oar -like cilia. The gluttonous Didinium is a fierce predator, and can eat other protists larger than its body. Graceful Euglena can move by means of whiplike flagella, but contains green chloroplasts like a plant. This is a strange and wonderful world is truly a marvelous expe-rience, and will surely alter the world view of anyone who enters it.

Look closely. Even a ten-power hand lens reveals more unseen worlds. The delicate spore cases waving above moss plants fire repro-ductive spores into the air. A myriad of tiny decomposers going about their business in a rotting log doggedly break down what once lived to make it available for others. Get in close. Crawl if you must. Lose yourself in a world unrevealed except to those who make the effort to penetrate its mysteries.

Creel Memories

UP UNTIL A few days ago, I had never caught a wild stream trout in Wisconsin. Having been teacher in western Colorado for 7 years, I was spoiled by the large, open streams throughout the iconic western slope of the Rockies, and the hundreds of lakes atop Grand Mesa. Needless to say, as a near penniless beginning teacher, I provided as much wild meat as possible for my family. It was a time of few "No Trespassing" signs, and frequent forays with students who knew the holes where trout were plentiful. Some could even reach in the creek and feel for them lodged in rocks, and throw them up on the bank. These kids taught me the ropes of stream trout fishing for meat.

It has been many, many years since I have fished those waters. One thing I do remember, is that, on my first introduction to Plateau Creek, I was not prepared to bring my catch home in a proper creel. I used a flexible branch, and it worked just fine.

Fast forward about thirty years. I decided to settle in the unique environs of the Driftless area after retirement. I saw tiny creeks as part of a topography left over from the last glaciers. They looked intimidating!

Just about wide enough to jump across, they wind their way through tangles of brush, weeds, and ticks that caused me to shy away for many years. It seemed one would have to e part animal to venture into those tunnels of vegetation that tore at clothing and made casting all but impossible.

I could not have been more wrong. A retired DNR warden and fellow taxidermist agreed to show me some honey holes he had helped enhance in years past. A brief ten minute drive from my home, and here we were on opening day, not seeing another soul on these clear flowing streams. While the water was a bit high and turbid that day, I went back when it was not. It took me no more than 5 casts to land three fine brown trout. My fishing was over by eight in the morning. Unprepared as usual, I tore off a flexible branch to use as a stringer, as I have always done. They work just fine.

I plan to commemorate this baptism into my return to trout angling. It will be a stringer mount of sorts, with three trout threaded on a flexible limb. In size, they are not exceptional. In my mind and heart, they are extraordinary. Life has come full circle. Once a young man fascinated at the ever extraordinary world of fishing in the Rockies, now the old man with fishing pole and walking stick plies the waters of Coulee country. The hills here are not mountains, but inspiring and complex in their biologic diversity. With hands and legs stiff from pain that comes with age, it is time to plod on. As the world rushes by on asphalt ribbons nearby, I am reborn in the first light of day. I am the young man once more.

Yerba de Primavera

IT IS TIME for the porky, mangy, denned-up bear to awaken. That bear is me. Like any other right-thinking beast, I envision green shoots and the bounty nature provides in abundance. Seed catalogs come way too early, but stir in me a foraging instinct I have possessed since childhood. It may be too early for my garden, but it will soon be time for scrounging the fields and forests for what they provide in abundance.

I am always amazed at what all stays green under the snow and ice. Most of these mosses and ground huggers are no good for eating, but that will soon change. Early on, spikes of cattails thrust upwards to the sun. I pull them up so as not to break off the tender blanched bases. Boiled and salted with butter, they are very close to asparagus. As ferns emerge, the coiled fiddleheads emerge and are a delicacy relished around the world. As time goes on, the plant kingdom marches forth with more and more choices, each with its prime time for harvest.

Although asparagus is not a native wild plant, who does not love seeing it burst forth after a rain and warm spell? It has gone feral. It is great from the garden, but even better when I can steal it for free. Its home is undisturbed ground such as fence lines, old railroad grades. I have the uncanny ability to be driving 60 mph and slam on the brakes when I see a few spears that would go unnoticed by all but a few. You will have to deal with like-minded competitors out there, but hauling a few meals with from a fence line feels almost like robbing a bank. Hit and run! Do not do this along Prindle road as a certain clan there is sure to hunt you down like a dog if they see you.

As the days warm a bit, wild onions sway with the grasses. These are potent, and much like garlic, a few go a long ways. If you are lucky enough to locate a patch of watercress in a spring-fed creek, you are in for one of the healthiest treats in nature. Like an aquatic spinach, the flavor is out of this world. I prefer to cook it for one reason only........I don't even like to say the words "parasitic flukes" that can invade your liver, but yes, do not eat it raw.

Another wild spinach is violets. As pretty as they are, the leaves can be used like spinach, and all parts of the plant are edible. What a lovely garnish it makes as a creamed dish with its purple flowers garnishing the goodly mound of vegetable.

What is a weed but a plant growing where we do not want it for some reason. Young dandelions are a tad bitter, but mixed in a salad, just like endive. In the ethnic Italian neighborhoods I grew up in, there were always folks of Mediterranean descent filling bags with them in the Spring. Supposedly a good "blood purifier" whatever that means.

Mint is all over, particularly in moist areas. It makes a great tea. Your cats will love you for it, since catnip is a mint and they don't seem to be picky about what type of mint it is. Make sure to pick enough and learn how to make a mojito!

Finally, at the edge of summer, a roadside weed known as lambs quarter fills the land. It has a slight garlic taste and is perfect to add to salads. It is easy to identify, and you can pick the leaves for a long time.

To denigrate these healthy plants by ignoring them or calling them "weeds" is a shame. Learn them by shape and habit and name. There is a deep satisfaction to adding these to your diet of beer and brats, thinning your blood for the coming summer, and awakening your hibernating soul again.

Shadow Cats

BACK IN THE early nineties, my blood ran hot each opening day of archery season, and generally for the next few months. I had permission to hunt a very productive woodlot, along with a few other fellows, and spent as much time as I could sitting in a tree stand during the glorious days of September and October. With all senses tuned to picking up the telltale presence of a deer, it was impossible not to hear a strangely wild growl that seemed out of place. Far in the distance, there was a distinct roar penetrating the darkness. I reasoned quickly it was not the ultimate buck grunt. I could not place it at all. For the most part, it sounded like something from a documentary on African big cats. For a moment, the reptilian part of my brain shot adrenaline into every fiber, and I became the Neanderthal facing saber tooth cat. The sound has a very unnerving effect on you when you consider our ancestors were prey. It hits you right in the gut and makes you want to be somewhere else. It was so contradictory. I could not use logic to figure this one out. I wanted to hop back in my vehicle, and made my way to it a bit more quickly than usual, waving my flashlight wildly back and forth and hoping not to catch a massive pair of glowing eyes staring back at me.

I mentioned this to a couple of my hunting partners who were from the area. It turns out Wisconsin is one of five states that allow citizens to own large, exotic cats. Bad idea. Nearby in Sharon Wisconsin, there is a sanctuary and retreat for animals that used to be in circus acts, or had to be abandoned by owners. So, I had indeed been hearing a group of lions at feeding time. What a relief. The retreat is known as Valley of the Kings and is still in operation. For years as I occupied my stand, I fancied myself deep in the African bush, waiting and watching for footfalls too silent to hear.

The thumps in the night do not end here. A few years back, a distanced myself from a barber who told me the story of a local black "panther." He knew I was a writer, and perhaps thought I was a fool. No records of any such critter. I unfriended this guy and have never gone back for a haircut. The audacity. Then a true friend who allows me to hunt some of the most wild country in Wisconsin told me he too had seen a black cougar. On a recent television show, the explanation became clear. While a black phase known as melanism is fairly common among jaguars and leopards, it is not among cougars. My thoughts now are, perhaps someone who legally raised and sold these exotic cats might have allowed a few to go feral to prowl the vast local forests.

Finally, at the beginning of the 2020 bear season, just a few miles from my home in the Merrillan area, an eleven year old girl shot probably the largest black bear ever taken in Wisconsin. Its estimated weight was over eight hundred pounds! Included in the hunt were trail cam pics of wolves chasing the bruin off a bait pile. I can only smile. I really do live in the backwoods.

Lions Of Tsavo

In black around you now we lie
The night, our mother gives no clue
Our glowing eyes are watching you

Out there, around you, can't you see
Or feel our heavy breathing near
Are crackling embers all you hear?

Your fire is comfort to you we know
A guardian from the secret foes
That stalk you now on silent paws
With padded steps we near, we two
Our glowing eyes are watching you

Think your fires strikes fear in us
Are canvas walls a fortress strong?
Sleep now, the night is young, and long

But later when the camp's asleep
In pitchy dead of dark we'll creep
Down dank ravine, 'cross misty veldt
Our feline presence now is felt

Look up, too late we're at your side
And not a thing that you can do
Our glowing eyes are watching you.

Happy Hunting Grounds

MY BEST MALE friend and former student, Zack Stanley, just shared a video with me on Facebook. Not my brand of music, but the lyrics and video itself were captivating. Images showed a group of folks either on the last day of their lives, or in the process of dying and reflecting on their lives. Bad circumstances, bad endings. Part way through, a crowd seems drawn to a glowing hole in the ground. They enter one end as they were, and emerge transformed. Okay, let's say heaven. It is a moving production.

Tree stands and fishing boats give one many opportunities to ponder life, its end, and the hereafter. In Native American cultures, we often hear of a belief in the "happy hunting grounds." While some evidence supports this concept, other sources do not. Many, many tribes existed before the white invasion, and their beliefs were as varied as the wildflowers on the plains. In fact, for some, the afterlife was viewed as a continuation of one's present life. The concept of Hell did not exist. I must concur, especially as one who has lived the outdoors life as hunter, fisherman, and forager. What evil could I possibly do in one lifetime that would sentence me to eternal torment? On the other hand, eternal bliss even seems like it would get old, say after a million years more or less.

So, if we do pass to the Happy Hunting Grounds, do we do so as we were when death overtook us? Would we be transformed into our youthful peak of prowess? Would our hunting endeavors be without challenge, roaming a land filled with ever-abundant game? Would all our shots be unerring? This is hard to comprehend. Where is the thrill if all needs are fulfilled? If there is no challenge, where is the joy of success? The struggles of life and figuring out how to survive them allow our appreciation.

I suppose it is all Yin and Yang. A warm campfire has no meaning unless you have been bitten by the cold. The taste of hunted and gathered food has no flavor without the arduous process of obtaining it and experiencing true hunger. Is this part of what makes a shore lunch seem like the best meal you ever ate?

Years ago, most likely in early college, I wrote a poem about a man with similar convictions. Yes, it is a bit trite, but still bears presenting.

Walleye Bill

I am a lazy old lug they say
Loafing and dreaming, fishing most days
You say I runnin' from reality
Mister, what's real for you ain't real for me
You see, I've been livin' all these years
Life for me ain't no veil of tears
I know there's a Maker, just don't know his name
Yet take time to ponder the whisper of rain
So I'll take a boat, some flopping fish and beer
Can't be no better place than here.

It would be nice if there was something like a Happy Hunting Ground, but like most, I doubt it. Ditto for the realm of eternal damnation. You can come close to Hell though if you have hunted grouse for very long. I would love to see all my hunting partners, human and animal again. After these many years of life, my only realization remains that, on a good day in the outdoors, I have walked hallowed ground. Heaven is right here.

We live many lives
They happen all at once.

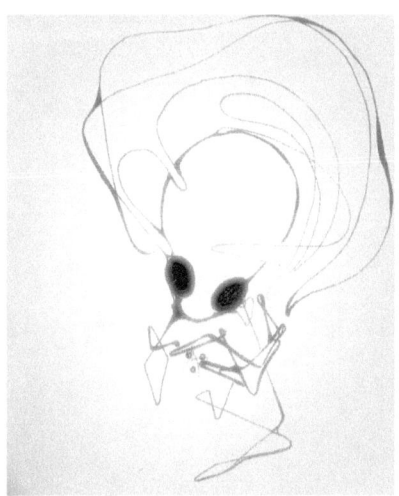

Under The Ashes

How they thrust order into that world of theirs
With lines
Slicing along courses
No river ever followed

Someday
Others will come from afar
Dusting, probing, picking at those lines

Revealing
How a people once moved forward
Always forward
With the precision of a troupe of nightcrawlers
Slicked out on pavement
After a summer rain.

Plastic trash
Gold of the past
Weightless wonder
A perfect gift
We throw it away.

Goals

I CAN ONLY guess how many articles on New Year's resolutions have been penned over the past few weeks. Some are humorous; others involve movie stars and celebrities. We need to peek into their lives, or do we?

Many of us will actually stride into the beginning of 2004 with this list of goals in hand, for we live in a society obsessed with goals. As a high school student, I felt proud to be characterized as a "goal-oriented" young man by a counselor. This of course, was meant to be a positive statement. Yet, with each passing year I became less and less inclined to get too serious about such lists. At one point, I remember making a statement I thought was profound at the time. It involved my goal of having no goals.

This of course is an impossibility. Even wishing to have no goals is a goal. Somehow though, I found a certain logic in this. Bits and pieces of what I considered wisdom seemed to reinforce in my mind this idea of easing off goal-directed behavior. Thoreau's advice to "simplify, simplify" rang true. In many religions, the giving up of earthly possessions and meditation in a wilderness setting is considered spiritually strengthening.

In 1995, I read a book authored by James Ogilvy entitled *Living Without a Goal,* and was convinced this would crystallize all these jumbled ideas about goallessness. It was a good read, but I was certainly in no position to tramp off into the mountains and become a monk or hermit.

However, it seems the times I was closest to this were the times of greatest happiness. Children seem happier than most adults, and perhaps it is because of their lack of heavy responsibilities. There were summer days when, as a beginning teacher, I chose to forget responsibilities, jump in the Jeep with a fishing rod and just drive up the mountain. I was not certain I would catch fish, or even where I was going other than up. I would not have to work at my job for another few months, so I could stay up late, sleep late and pretty much do whatever I wanted. It was during these long summer days when I could again become like a child. While others slogged to the workplace each day, I could do as I pleased.

Even hunting and fishing has become much less about the goal of bagging a trophy. It is an excuse to slip back into that world of the present, forget about what needs to be done tomorrow, and experience the enthusiasm of a child seeing the world for the first time. In this state of mind, every hooked fish is as exciting as the first. Every flushed bird startles the heart, and like a magnifying glass, focuses the moment.

So this year, rather than rattling off a list of resolutions I will probably not keep, I will make it a priority to simplify more things. I will let go of more responsibilities when I can. I will make an effort to turn my outdoor meanderings into meditations rather than pursuits. I will try to keep the words of Ogilvy in my mind, and repeat them like mantras if necessary. At the end of his book, he gives the following advice:

"Give up the goal of wealth. You probably have as much money as you need. Let go of the goal of self-sufficiency. You will never achieve it, and will destroy your relationships with others while trying. Give up the goal of independence. The world does not work that way. Give up the gold of true love. Love, if it is romantic, is never, strictly speaking, true. And if it is not romantic, it is not true love. Let go of the goal of happiness. That bird lights only when least expected. Let go of the goal of fame. Its concave mirror distorts as it amplifies."

It seems to have taken a lifetime of being feverishly goal-oriented to get myself into a position of being able to let some of them go. Most of those things I labored so diligently to achieve have been accomplished. There is no need for a newer car, bigger home, or smarter-looking wardrobe. While I may be wrong about the wardrobe, let's just say I feel it is healthier to want less stuff. I have yet to dig for clams, hunt the tundra, or spend a night on the Amazon. I get a sense I will do all of these, but not on some agenda, or especially not on someone else's. These are more thoughts than goals, more dreams than plans. I will make more time to meditate on these things, and how to erase as much accumulated clutter in my life as possible. If this is itself a goal, at least it is a worthy one.

Letting Go

It was not so much the forest I missed
but that one certain tree
a smaller piece of me
had clawed his way up
cradled by arms older,
stronger than my own
An awkward bird
feeling the eagle inside
poised to fly
where such trees do not flourish
and I could not follow.

The noise we now make
Echoes against a future without us.

A Roach in my World

YESTERDAY, AS I was painting in my basement studio, I chanced to look over at an absolutely humongous cockroach perched happily on a warm rock. Now, in case you have surmised that I live in some kind of filthy hovel, rest assured I do not. My Madagascar hissing cockroach is more than two inches long, a true giant of its species. It is a male, with protruding horns on its head. Although it has wings, it does not fly. When prodded or disturbed in any way, it belches out a menacing hiss.

I took a break from my work to stare at the creature. It had been awhile since I fed him, so I got him all stirred up by introducing some bok choy leaves to his confined world. After a brief nibble, he slowly crawled back to sit motionlessly atop his sizzle stone.

Creatures this alien evoke a special kind of wonder in me. What is their purpose? Why do I have the dumb thing in my basement anyway? What is my purpose? How are we the same, and are we different?

Despite the obvious answers relating to physiology, intelligence, placement on the evolutionary ladder, then question of purpose still haunts me.

Yes, I know why I purchased this particular insect. I kept it in my classroom and took it out now and then for students to handle. The idea was to let them overcome aversions to creepy-crawlies, and perhaps even come to appreciate "bugs" and other invertebrates that most of us see as a nuisance.

Now that I have retired from teaching, it seems nobody wanted to house this refined product that has survived on this planet much longer than humans. It seems my insect comrade has outlived its role in life. Then again, he has me sitting here questioning my own purpose.

Oh, of course I can find solace in the fact I have contributed to the education of many students over the years. I still feel I have contributions to make through artwork and writing. Yet, I often feel as insignificant as my buddy the roach. I wish I had more faith in some grand purpose for all of us. Perhaps we carry on just because we can.

Still, I feel I learned a bit of a lesson through this experience. While I understand my purpose for having had that ungainly creation in my classroom, he was unaware of it.

At a time in life when I hope to devote more time to spiritual issues and meditations, this was a bit of a revelation. Could it be that, what I can only address as the Creator, has a reason for the existence of everything that I could be totally unaware of? Looking at this tiny corner of my basement as a microcosm of the universe, it appears so.

In the words of Einstein, "I see a pattern, but I cannot imagine the maker of the pattern. I see a clock, but I cannot envision the clockmaker. The human mind is unable to conceive of the four dimensions, so how can it conceive of a God, before whom a thousand years and a thousand dimensions are as one?"

Some day, as an old man, perhaps I will spend most of my time sitting on my own version of a warm rock, staring into the distance with few responsibilities. Will I then feel I lack a purpose? Will I become just another creature that consumes oxygen and returns carbon dioxide to the environment?

Unlike my roach, I hope that by immersing myself in that natural world, away from the fleeting contrivances of man, I will better understand the purpose and immensity of the tapestry of life around me.

Without effort, I will crawl from my rock to my food and foraging with a smile, hopefully understanding more than I do now.

Scent Silliness

WE ALL KNOW that deer and most other wild mammals are masters at detecting scents that strike a panic button. Evidently, human stench is one of the scariest. Like most hunters, I give scent control some thought. I take a leisurely bath at least once a week. I abstain from Old Spice cologne or Axe deodorant before the hunt. Topping off my gas tank involves great care not to splash any on my camo clothing, in spite of the fact that breakfast was from the gas station. What is wrong with pepperoni pizza for breakfast and using my sleeve for a napkin?

Hey, there is no way not to stumble into odors. Last time I cleaned and put my hunting clothes in a "scent proof" plastic bag, my wife decided they could use a dose of Febreeze. The way I figure it, those masters of marketing have plenty of products guaranteed to eliminate my over-whelming stench. I cannot help wondering though, each time I am tempted to purchase one, if they really work. Stink destroying laundry soap is supposed to be the place to start. Whoaaaa.......that stuff is pricey. Is it any better than plain old non-scented soap? Spray on scent block-ers are supposed to neutralize human odor. I cannot help but wonder if they really do. My in-depth experience gives me reason to believe they do not. There are scent killer deodorants, body wipes, fabrics, and even chewing gum to keep your mouth fresh as a pine forest.

On top of all this, there are cover scents. Yeah, I spray a bit of doe pee on a drag and pull it around my hunting paths at times. I am told this has a shelf life, but always hate to throw away a collection of partially-empty bottles from years gone by. After awhile, it doesn't smell like urine at all. More like straight up ammonia. I don't bother with the earth scent or pine potpourri. Pretty sure I could just use pine needles and dirt. You can just step on a fresh cow pie as well.

In case one is still getting busted by wary old bucks, let's not forget attraction scents. When baiting was not legal in my zone, I tried a product that was supposed to "cornfuse" deer into believing they were headed for a pile of corn. Smelled just like a giant box of buttered popcorn. Then of course there is the apple scent that reminds me of a Jolly Rancher hard candy. Nothing at all like real apples. It never hurts to spritz a bit of acorn scented "rage" inducing feed into a bait pile. Even more high tech is a product that is supposed to "jam" the ability of a buck to scent you. Yeah, for sure. Maybe a forest fire?

Just on the long shot you might be one of those hunters that might bring a responsibly sized nip of firewater with you in your flask, I can only imagine how far away wildlife can dial in on that. Heck, if I can smell my hunting buddy half a block away.........well, go figure. But on a philosophical closing note, if you are going to have a snort to cut the morning cold, my choice is Jaegermeister. It does have a picture of a deer on the bottle, so, there must be some reason, eh?

We can all be delivered by silliness
What a wonderful gift!

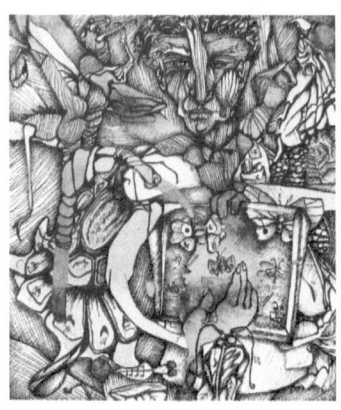

My Walking Stick

DESPITE OUR BEST intentions, we all slip and fall. This propensity seems to increase exponentially with a person's age. Throw in an artificial hip and gimpy, arthritic knee, and you will be just like me. Years ago, after my first hip surgery, I learned to walk very, very carefully during my times afield. The consequences of dislocation or breakage are daunting. Unlike the young bucks in commercials, I cannot vault off the back of a pickup anymore. Yet, I continue to get out as much as possible and hike, hunt mushrooms, and scout new hunting grounds.

I have been using long staff for a long time, and actually feel uncomfortable without it. Not to be confused with a short cane, a staff allows you to instantly grip it if you feel yourself going down. A cane will not do this. Mine is 47 inches long with a knobby end on it almost like an Irish shillelaghs, which were useful weapons in their time. The longer Japanese staff known as a bo, is a devastating weapon in trained hands. Additionally, canes are one weapon you can take on a plane and not be denied. A rubber tip protects the wood and is useful on civilized tile floors. In winter, I add a short spike for gripping ice.

The hilly Coulee region of Wisconsin has plenty of wet roots that just beg to be slipped on. A good staff can help you catch yourself and avert a tragedy. Getting in and out of a boat in shallow water is made much simpler with this "extra leg" to balance on. Need a shooting stick? A screw hole in one end will allow an attachment perfect for a monopod. If you want to get a bit crazier, there are spear points, frog gigs, and other sharp things that you can modify your all- purpose tool with.

While there are high tech aluminum, adjustable models out there, I prefer my wooden wacker. While there are many strong woods, I can highly recommend wax wood or rattan. Almost unbreakable, and you can get long lengths that can be modified in the wax wood. I have a few simple carvings on mine. Escrima stick masters in the Orient use a torch to burn designs on their devastating fighting sticks. The look is very nice, and has a camo effect like a leopard.

A well- designed and balanced long staff will be a friend for sure. It will save some wear and tear on your knees, add to your upper body workout, and makes a great fish club for those pesky and slimy pike hopping around the floor of your boat. It can teach cantankerous farm dogs that like to nibble at your leg flesh an enduring lesson. But one or make one, there will come a time when you will be glad you did.

There is no such thing
As a flower out of place.

Buddha

HOTAI HAS BEEN a kind friend to me for most of my life. His carved likeness is an inspiration in times of melancholy. He smiles eternally. His youth, hair, and manly posture are gone. He holds his few meager belongings in a bag slung over one shoulder. I cannot know what brightness he sees down the road that is making him smile, but he gazes ahead with boundless optimism.

The older I become, the more I relate to my laughing Buddha. There are times it is best to lay down ones bag of possessions, worries, and negativity. Times to stop and meditate on the fact that, I too have most of my life behind me, and am not in the shape I used to be. It is easy to look at young folks and be envious of their physical prowess and energy. They have a longer road ahead of them, while mine grows shorter, and the steps more difficult.

Hotai is a reminder that "the meaning of life is to find meaning in life." As I hold him and rub his drooping belly for good luck, part of me knows what he sees, and the things that make him smile. I often picture him stopping to ponder some small bird chasing an insect, or sitting on the shore of a lake gazing at yet another sunset. Unlike myself, he seems comfortable with his ponderous body, and opens his robe to the breeze to feel the elements against his bare skin, without the least bit of self- consciousness.

Here is a being that can chortle up a belly laugh from deep within. He has lived long enough to have experienced just about all he needs to. Less and less ties him to the "monkey mind" chatter that dominates life for so long. The background noise is quiet now, and he is allowed time to do as he pleases. He seems to be on the brink of something like retirement, but he is far from slacking off. In whatever time Buddah has left, there will be adventures to be relished that were always too short in younger years. Simple bowls of soup can now be savored without interruption. Kneeling on the warm, earth to nurture garden plants has evolved into a meditation ritual. Simple work is no longer work, but prayer.

I like to imagine my diminutive sage has finally come to grips with the realities of where life has taken him, and doors that have, in all probability, closed. Hotai still putters at things like playing guitar and fly fishing. He has never truly mastered either of these talents, but still revels in such pursuits. It is far too late to become a proficient golfer. Skiing is off the list of interests as well. Old worn legs can only do so much. The time for learning complex recreational pursuits is over.

So what is packed in his bag? Most likely some simple food, like jerky and peanuts. A pencil and paper to write down reminders and the thoughts of an old man. Gloves for the cold, and a woolen hat. Colorful rocks and shells jostle around a few coins and sweet, hard candies. A small tin of tea leaves is a constant companion. There is no compass, since the Buddha is not certain where his path takes him. He will live through the compassion of others and his own wit and wile, never packing more than he requires, except a length of weighted line and some hooks.

One cannot tell by looking at Hotai where he has been, or the life experiences behind him. As we say these days, his visage bears the signs of a being moving forward. Weather and difficult trails do not deter his enthusiasm for life, since he has experienced the gamut of what a man can do. These days, the sublime pleasure of simple things is all that remains. Things that were overlooked by a younger man wrapped in the ambitions of youth. Life boils down to a warm bowl of rice with tea, watching birds, and foraging in the thicket. Even peeing in the woods affords a wisp of satisfaction. There is always water and wind to listen to. Now and then, thoughts of a woman or two from the past bring a smile to his face. Telling embellished old stories to children brings out his best. For those who admonish others to live in the present, Buddha understands that, while the past is past, his present is bound to every moment of that past.

Water and food
Water and food
They are never for want
Not knowing
Who their God is.

RECIPES

Gardening has always been a passion, and so has the preparation of healthy, delicious food. Soups were often the starters for the day. Scratch soups packed with fresh vegetables. Growing up in a heavily Italian neighborhood gave an appreciation for specialties like banya cauda, giardiniera, and pasta dishes. As a kid, I tried everything and savored exotic dishes, especially oriental food. As an adult, many happy months were spent in Puerto Aventuras Mexico, where the farmers market was a huge cornucopia of fresh mangoes, papaya, chaya, and so many root crops. I will sometimes share a quickie version of a recipe that was often used in a pinch. As I have had some health concerns in my latter years, I am familiar with ways to help. No sugar here. I use Stevia and a tiny bit of molasses for brown sugar. Many items would be in line with Mediterranean diets.

Being a backwoods forager, some ingredients may seem alien, but they are all readily available even in urban environments. Comfort foods are family staples that hearken back to my youth, and will never be forgotten.

ANASAZI BEANS

These black and white beans are the same ones grown by the Anasazi people in our American southwest. The pattern on them looks like a yin-yang symbol. They taste great and cook a bit faster than some beans, but these heirlooms are just cool to munch down on thinking of their ancestry. Use as you would in any scratch bean recipe.

6 cups cooked beans
1/2 lb lean burger
1 clove minced garlic
1 small chopped onion
2 Tbs brown sugar
2 Tbs molasses
1 Tbs cider vinegar
1 tsp dry mustard

4 pieces fried bacon crumbled
    with drippings
1 chopped apple
1 diced pepper
1 small can fire roasted chiles or
    plain chiles (chopped fine)
2 Tbsp barbecue sauce, dry rub,
    or any seasoning you like.

Mix all ingredients in a bean pot or large casserole dish.Cook 1 hr at 375 degrees. Great with cornbread.

BABA GANOUSH

I tend to grow too many eggplant. It is overall one of the healthiest foods one can eat. Sliced, breaded and fried is how I had it as a kid, and still a favorite. Here is a dip with Middle Eastern origins that is great on warm pita bread or just about anything else. Try it, if for no other reason than to say "Baba Ganoush."

1 eggplant
1/4 cup lemon juice
1/4 cup tahini (in a pinch you
   can use peanut butter thinned
   with some sesame oil.)

2 Tbsp sesame seeds
1 1/2 Tbsp olive oil
1 - 2 cloves garlic
salt and pepper to taste

Roast an eggplant that has been cut in half lengthwise. Leave skin on. 400 degrees at about 30 minutes. Grilling is even faster and gives a sublime smokey taste. Scoop out the mushy, cooked eggplant.

Place everything in a blender and puree. Transfer to a bowl and refrigerate for 3 hours.

BANYA CAUDA

I first tried this as a teen. My Sicilian Aunt Gloria made this every New Year's Eve. Simple and sooooo tasty! Get a good, crusty rustic bread or baguette and dip as you eat. Amazing.

3/4 stick of butter   4 cloves of finely chopped garlic
16 oz. container of sour cream   3/4 cup olive oil
12 anchovy fillets

Heat in a frying pan on medium while stirring. Ingredients will dissolve and blend into each other. Keep on low heat for dipping.

FISH CHOWDER

Always near the top of my list of comfort foods is clam and fish chowder. For real clam chowder, the minced stuff does not cut it. Big, fat steamed cherrystone clams do. For fish, the lean firm types are best. Fillets from panfish work perfectly.

1 1/2 pounds of fish chunks	4 oz thick bacon
1 cup clam juice or fish broth	1 bay leaf
3 cups half and half (can have heavy cream mixed in)	2 celery stalks chopped fine 1/2 cup white wine
1 large onion chopped	1 Tbsp fresh thyme
2 Tbsp butter	2 Tbsp chopped parsley
1 lb potatoes cut in 3/4 in cubes	1 tsp Old Bay spice or paprika

Saute onions and bacon in a Tbsp of oil. Remove bacon to paper towels.Add wine, simmer until it reduces by 1/2.Add potatoes, butter, celery, herbs and spice to the mix. Simmer until potatoes are done. 10 min.Heat cream and half and half in a separate pan. Do NOT boil. Add fish on top of potatoes. Cook on simmer until fish is opaque and done. (10 min) Add cream, half and half and bacon. Return to simmer. Add salt and pepper to taste. Garnish with parsley to serve. Don't forget the hot sauce!

Quick cheat......add some fish and bacon bits to a can of hearty chowder.

MOM'S BEST ON THE PLANET EGGPLANT SOUP

This is a soup everybody loves. As are all my soups, hearty and healthy.

1 peeled eggplant diced in
   1 inch pieces
2 sliced of diced carrots
2 diced potatoes
1 diced onion
2 diced tomatoes (you can use
   canned diced tomatoes or
   Rotel)

5 beef bouillon cubes
4 cups water
1 Tbsp., grated Parmesan or
   Romano cheese
1 tsp brown sugar
1 Tbsp dried oregano

Bring to boil and allow to simmer until carrots are soft. Experiment by adding hot peppers, V8 juice, celery, or your choice.

TOP 10 LEAST FAVORITE WARDEN RECIPES

10. Bird of prey shish-ka-bob.

9. Marijuana food plot burned out doe.

8. 00 buckshot turkey pate

7. Ground swatted grouse

6. Trespass teal tidbits

5. Pellet gunned owl drumsticks

4. Steamed undersized trout

3. DNR citation sauced duck

2. Summer season pheasant nuggets

And the number one Least Favorite Warden Recipes.........

1. Poached venison.

GIARDINIERA

A staple relish for anything Italian, especially sandwiches and salads. You can buy the jars, but making it is easy. With fresh garden vegetables, this has no equal. Real Chicago style!

6 cups assorted diced peppers
1 celery stalk, diced
1 carrot, diced
1 small onion, diced
3/4 cup cauliflower florets, diced
2 cloves fresh garlic, chopped finely
1 1/2 Tbsp dried oregano

1/2 tsp black pepper
1 cup sliced and chopped green olives
1 cup white vinegar
1 cup olive oil (canola works)
1/2 cup kosher salt (or non-iodized)

Put veggies in a non-reactive bowl, add salt and water, cover and place in the fridge overnight.

Drain, rinse, add oil, vinegar, and spices. Refrigerate for a day or 2. No fuss with canning. Stays fresh and crisp for weeks if refrigerated. I have eaten it this way for as long as a year later......but hey, keep it real.

KOHLATATO SOUP

I love fresh kohlrabis! One of the healthiest and most versatile vegetables. Sadly, many folks have never tried them. One of the best ways
is sliced, salted, and raw. Here is a soup that cuts down on the carbs
in potatoes, and mixes them with other garden treats.

1 pack Knorr cream of leek soup

2 cups peeled and diced
kohlrabis

2 cups peeled and diced potatoes

1 cup diced zucchini

1 small diced onion

1/2 cup white wine

2 Tbs parmesan or romano
cheese

half and half or heavy cream to
taste

Make the Knorr soup according to directions. Add cooked veggies,
wine, and cheese to this. To thicken, use half and half or cream with
corn starch or flour and water to get a thicker consistency. A dash of
curry powder may be to your liking. Experiment!

LUPINI SNACKS

Giant jars of these used to stand in every real Italian grocery store. One of the healthiest snacks imaginable. High in fiber, low in net carbs. A snack that has been around since ancient Egypt and Rome. These beans are extremely bitter when dry, so they go through numerous soaks to leach that out. Worth every minute you put into them, and they keep for a long time refrigerated.

1 lb dry Lupini beans   water
Kosher salt (or non-iodized salt)

Cover dry beans with water in a non-reactive container. Soak overnight. Drain and boil for 45 min. Drain and rinse a couple times each day for 6 or seven days. Taste. If still bitter, keep up the drain and rinse routine. Add salt to taste and leave it in the water. This mix does not have to be refrigerated for weeks. If you wish to refrigerate later, that is fine. Really Mediterranean if you mix in with some olives and eat together with the beans. Some pop the beans out of their skins by squeezing them, many like the skins as well. Fiber, fiber, fiber.

PEA SOUP AND NECK BONES

16 oz dry split peas
1 cup diced onion
1/2 cup diced carrot
1/2 cup diced celery
6 cups ham or chicken stock

1/2 clove of garlic (optional)
1 bay leaf
1-2 Tbsp nutmeg
1 lb smoked meat

Boil the broth, peas, veggies and seasonings. Smoked neck bones, pork hocks, turkey wings or thighs. In fact, any of these will work, but smoked is best. Simmer on low for 45 minutes and check. Peas should begin to get smooth. When it is at the consistency you prefer, add a dash of pepper and salt to taste. The key ingredient here is nutmeg. It makes all the difference.

PEPPER SANDWICH

I was introduced to this Italian specialty by my Dad's boss, Nick Latoria of Franklin Park Illinois. He was always giving shells and rocks to me and my sister. A kind man with great humor.

No long list of ingredients here. Grill some long peppers like Anaheim, Poblano, or bullhorn types and put on a crisp Italian bread baguette. Add your favorite pasta sauce, a strip of sausage or hard salami, grated Romano, and any relish you enjoy so long as it is a nice, oily giardiniera.

PHEASANT OR GROUSE

Game birds can be dry and chewy. This recipe is truly a favorite and well worth the effort.

Mix a coating in a paper bag off 1/4 cup flour 1/8 tbs black pepper 1/4 tbs paprika 1/4 tbs thyme 1/4 tbs salt

Take game bird breasts and shake in a bag with mix until coated. Commercial mixes work well, just adde spices.

Brown the beasts in a mix of oil and 3 tbs butter . Set aside.

Drain frying oils and add 1/2 cup chicken broth, 1/2 cup white wine, 1-2 cloves and 2 tbs of raisins or cranberries.

Simmer 30 -40 min and pour over bird. (or do you simmer the browned breasts for 20-30 min?

Getting Pickled: Pickled Pike Recipes

The ice fishing, or "hard water," season here up north lasts a long time. Many tournaments are held in February, a good time to become distracted from cabin fever. It will not be long before the ice gradually returns to its liquid phase, but we are not there yet. As I write, an army of anglers still hunker over mysterious, dark holes in the ice, trying to divine the fate of their quarry below. Perhaps you have already stocked up on some juicy fillets and wonder how to best prepare them. Fish taken from icy-cold water are some of the finest eating. Most of these get beer-battered and served up as crispy hunks of goodness. Nothing quite like fresh fish!

However, there is another way to enjoy them, and that is pickling. Any fish can be pickled, but northern pike are some of the best. And, with tip-ups flying in the breeze, now is a perfect time to try your hand at this venerable method of preparation. Forget the herring you may have sampled in stores. Pike come out way tastier, and you can have fun experimenting with your own blend of spices.

If this is your first venture into pickling, you will be surprised at how easy it is. The results are goof-proof. The end product will keep for weeks and dissolves those pesky Y bones common to pike. Here are some tips to turn out a gourmet's delight.

First, fish need to be frozen at least four days. This destroys any parasites which may be present. Water should be high-quality drinking water. Tap water high in hardness, iron, or other minerals can give an off flavor. If this sounds like your tap water, use bottled water. Vinegar is another key ingredient. White vinegar with an acid content of 5 percent is best and will not give the fish an off color. Vinegar at the recommended levels helps prevent bacterial growth. Salt should be the pickling or canning variety. It should not be iodized. Plain table sugar is used as a sweetening agent. Artificial sweeteners work too.

With those basics at hand and your fillets cut into chunks, it is time to pickle.

In a non-metal container, for each 5 pounds of fish, dissolve 2-1/2 cups of salt into one gallon of water. Refrigerate for 48 hours. This is called brining. Rinse the brined fish in cold water and cover with undiluted White vinegar for another 24 hours. This further firms up the flesh and dissolves tiny bones. Now, it is time to pack the fish in jars. Place chopped onions in the bottom and top of the jar before covering with one of the following pickling solutions.

Herring Style

(for 5 pounds of fish)

1 quart distilled vinegar	4 teaspoons of pickling spice
5 1/2 cups sugar	1 cup dry white wine

Combine these ingredients (except the wine) and bring to a boil. When cool, add the wine and place scalded lids on your jars. Refrigerate a week before eating. These should keep six to eight weeks in the fridge.

Mustard Pickle

(for 5 pounds of fish)

1 cup vegetable oil
3 cups distilled vinegar
1/3 cup prepared mustard
1/2 cup sugar

1 tsp ground white pepper
1 tsp pickling spice
3 bay leaves

Mix these and bring to a boil. When cool, fill jars with the solution and onions. Cover with scalded lids and refrigerate a week before sampling.

Joe Jackowski's Ultimate Pickle

Step 1

1 qt cut and skinned fish
1 cup White vinegar

5/8 cup pickling (canning) salt

Place in large jar and let stand in fridge covered for 7 days. Shake once a day.

Step 2

On day 8, rinse with cold water until water runs clear. Let stand in cold water for 1 hour.

Step 3

Slice desired amount of small onions (yellow are best)

Step 4

In saucepan, mix:

1 cup White vinegar   1 cup sugar

Heat until sugar dissolves but don't boil

Add 1 cup of fruit wine (Boone's Farm or something made from apples or pears) and let cool.

Step 5

Drain water from step 2, add onions and cool mixture from step 4. Cover and let stand for 48 hours.

Enjoy your pickled pike!

SLOPPY DOE

A staple in any home. This sandwich begs for experimentation. Try. adding finely chopped giardiniera for any veggies, or even some relish. Hot ingredients are some of my favorites. Try some red pepper flakes, sri-racha sauce, and spices like oregano to give it that extra kick. Add a bit of wild game sausage to the ground meat to jazz it up as well. You cannot screw this one up.

1 lb ground venison
1 tsp brown sugar
1/4 cup chopped onion
1/4 cup chopped peppers (mild or hot to taste. A mix of red and green is appealing)

1 tsp prepared mustard
1/2 tsp garlic powder
3/4 cup tomato sauce
1 tsp Worchestershire sauce
2 tsp olive oil

Brown the venison with the oil . Drain oil. Add the other ingredients, simmer for 10 minutes or so. Salt and pepper to taste and serve on a sturdy bun.

VENISON STROGANOFF

Any recipe for beef stroganoff can be used for venison as well. I love throwing in thin slices of heart, plus cuts of steak tenderized and pounded thin with a mallet.

1 1/2 lbs venison (thin)
2 Tbsp oil
2 Tbsp butter
1 med. onion sliced
8 oz sliced fresh mushrooms (
   dried can be used, shiitake is
great)
1 can beef broth
1 can cream mushroom soup
1 cup sour cream
Cooked egg noodles

Add a bit of salt, pepper, a dash of garlic powder to the meat, dust with flour, brown quickly in a large skillet. Remove steak from pan. Add onion and mushrooms to the drippings. Saute a few minutes until onion is tender. Put steak back into pan and add add mushroom soup and beef broth. Cook on low 20 minutes covered.Stir in sour cream the last few minutes. Pour over noodles and serve.(Quick method.....use a package mix)

SUNCHOKE RELISH

Sunchokes, aka Jerusalem artichokes are native to our country, need no special care, and produce tons of tasty tubers underground. They spread on their own, so you can plant a few and will have a heavy row of them to harvest in a couple of years. Taste is a bit like a potato. Their starch will not spike blood sugar, so safe for diabetics. Deer like the leaves of this perennial, so they are great in food plots as well. It is said they can produce flatulence in some, so go easy Pancho!

1 qt chopped sun chokes (Don't try to peel them, just scrub well)

1 large onion (coarsely chopped)

2 large peppers (chopped) (multi-colored is nice)

2 Tbsp mustard seed

1 tsp celery seed

1/2 tsp turmeric

2 Tsp pickling spice in a bag

2 1/2 cups white vinegar

2 cups sugar (or equivalent sweetener)

3/4 tsp salt

Combine spices and seasonings in a non-reactive pan. Bring to boil. Add veggies simmer 10 minutes. Process as any salsa in a hot water bath 10 minutes.Store out of light (sunchokes darken in light) and let flavor develop for a week.

WILD RICE CREAMY AND COLD

Here is a must-try dish. Tasty and filling, it can be a main dish. Wild rice can be mixed with other rices and I like it with hulless barley. This hulless barley is NOT pearled barely. In fact, it is a different plant. It is chewy and should not spike blood sugar like processed barley. It is indeed whole grain.

6 oz wild rice or rice grain mix	1/2 cup mayo
1/2 up diced cucumber	1/4 cup plain yogurt
1 cup diced tomato	2 Tbsp chopped parsley
1 cup diced celery	dry roasted peanuts

Cook the grain mix. Add the rest of the ingredients. Top with parsley and peanuts. Salt and pepper to taste. Chill. Like many dishes, best after sitting a day.